# Preface

## 1. Who should use this book

This book is aimed at students on computing and business courses of all types, who need to learn how to use dBASE III or dBASE IV and have access to an IBM personal computer or compatible with either a dual floppy disk or hard disk system. dBASE is the industry-standard database management system for the IBM personal computers and compatibles.

Computing skills are more or less mandatory on all levels of business-related courses from GNVQ to degree, including courses in Finance, Tourism, Catering and Law. The learning material in this book requires minimal (or no) input from a lecturer and can be used as a self-instruction guide.

Three levels and types of business student are catered for:

❏ **Beginners** learning dBASE as part of an introduction to Business Computing, who need to perform simple but worthwhile tasks, e.g. creating small databases of information, querying them and displaying the results.

❏ **Intermediate students** – as skills and confidence develop, students can perform more complex tasks, e.g. designing their own screen layouts and printed reports, and working with multiple databases.

❏ **Advanced students** – students studying Business Computing as a major course component who need to program in dBASE.

The material used makes no assumptions about your previous experience of either computing or business.
Both the dBASE skills and their business applications are explained in simple terms.

## 2. Developments in dBASE

dBASE III was introduced in 1985, followed by dBASE IV in 1988. Despite the continued popularity of dBASE III, especially in education, many users have now changed to dBASE IV. This book covers both dBASE III, and dBASE IV from version 1.1. to 1.5.

Ashton-Tate, the original producers of dBASE, were taken over by their major competitor, Borland International Inc. in 1991. This gives Borland database products about 70% of the PC market. In 1992 Borland brought out dBASE IV 1.5, which replaces earlier versions. It remains fully DOS compatible and can be used with a mouse.

## 3. The scope of the book

There are already a number of textbooks on the market covering dBASE III or dBASE IV. For the most part they are expensive, often US produced textbooks, offering comprehensive coverage, and aimed mainly at the advanced student or the industry practitioner.

Of the few cheaper textbooks, none have addressed themselves to both versions of dBASE, or to all three levels of student mentioned above. None have covered all three modes – the menu-driven, command driven, and the programming modes of dBASE. This book covers all three.

A book of this size and price cannot be completely comprehensive, nor does it need to be. If computer literacy can be compared to learning a language, then one does not need to learn the complete contents of a dictionary to communicate effectively, one needs only the main vocabulary and grammar! Similarly the function of this book is to cover the *essentials* of dBASE at each level – *menu-driven*, *command driven*, and *programming*.

It will give students the confidence to perform the following essential tasks:

❐ Creating and searching a database

❐ Modifying and maintaining a database

❐ Indexing, reports and queries

❐ Programming fundamentals

❐ Printed reports, screen design and user menus

❐ Multiple databases

❐ Data validation and security

All the activities in this book are based around *business examples* and have been tested by the author on business HND and degree students. The dBASE features that best solve typical business problems have been included.
These features are introduced progressively by means of a series of student learning activities.

## 4. The structure of the book

This book is divided into three sections:

The dBASE III menu-driven mode, the 'Assist', is completely different in operation to the dBASE IV menu system, the 'Control Center'. For this reason each is given its own section (Sections 1 and 2). On the other hand both the dBASE command mode (the so-called 'dot prompt') and the programming mode share so many common features that they can be dealt with in the same section – Section 3.

## 5. Active-learning approach

The teaching/learning approach of this book departs from traditional textbook practice. dBASE features are introduced in the context of practical business activities and problems to be solved, with the opportunity for further independent practice and consolidation.

Each chapter is divided into a number of activities, and each activity is subdivided into:

❐ **Objectives**

Summary of objectives to be achieved and skills to be gained.

❐ **Introduction**

Explains the purpose of the activity (including, briefly, theoretical and business issues where appropriate).

❐ **Guided activity**

Step-by-step instructions to perform the skills.

❐ **Independent activity**

Follow-up activities with minimal or no instructions.

❐ **Summary of commands etc. used**

Quick reference to commands and function keys used in the activity.

Each activity, therefore, promotes active learning. It gives students maximum support during initial learning by use of guided activities, and encourages further reflection, theory and experimentation by independent activity. Students and/or lecturers will therefore be able to assess their progress.

## 6. Hints on active learning

Everyone learns at their own pace and in their own way; the following hints may be useful, whether you are learning independently or part of a lecturer-led group.

❐ Do not omit or 'jump around' between activities; each activity builds upon knowledge and skills previously gained.
You will also find that the dBASE applications that you develop require earlier applications to work.

❐ Be patient and work slowly and methodically, especially in the early stages when progress may be very slow.

❐ Try not to compare your progress with others too much. Fastest is not always best!

❐ Don't try to achieve too much in one session. Time for rest and reflection are important.

❐ Remember that you are learning by doing. Read the instructions carefully, study the effects your key strokes have on screen and ask yourself why.

❐ Mistakes are part of learning. No one can anticipate all the ones that you may make in this book. Again, consider the keys that you have pressed, and what is on the screen *before* making amendments, most mistakes are simple key press or typing errors.

❐ Make time to complete the independent exercises, especially if you are learning on your own. They are your best guide to your progress.

## 7. Lecturers' supplement

A copyright-free $3\frac{1}{2}$ (720k) disk is available which includes all the dBASE programs, databases, etc. used in this book for lecturers' reference/demonstration/checking of students' work etc. This disk is available free to all *lecturers* who adopt the book as a course text (please apply to the publishers on college headed notepaper).

*J. Muir*

# Contents

# Introduction

## 1. Databases in business

Since the microcomputer's initial impact on business in the 80's, three types of business software have emerged as industry standards, namely the word processor, the spreadsheet and the database management system. This is hardly surprising, as they fulfil three key business needs:

☐ All businesses need to cope with the volumes of text that they create – letters, memos, reports etc. – hence the word processor.

☐ They need to perform financial analysis – budgeting, cash flow projections, and financial management of all kinds – hence the spreadsheet.

☐ The third major need is to store and retrieve records of all types – stock, personnel, customer etc. – hence the need for database management systems.

The industry leader in computerised databases for the business micro or personal computer are dBASE III and dBASE IV produced by the US software house Ashton-Tate (now Borland). Since its inception with dBASE II in 1982, this family of programs has been progressively improved and expanded.

## 2. Database concepts and terminology

We all use databases either at home or in business, some computerised, some manual. An address book is an example of a simple manual *database*. It consists of a collection of related *records*, one for each individual or organisation; each record contains the same items of information or *fields* – name, address, telephone number and, perhaps, post code.

There are different *field types* – alphabetic, e.g. surname, and numeric, e.g. phone number. However, the contents of each field, the *field value* will be different for each record. The address book entries – the 'records' – are stored to make look-up and retrieval of this information easy. Usually the records are stored in some logical order for ease of access; for an address book this is the surname. The field used to order a database is known as the *key field*.

The total software package that creates and runs the database is the Database Management System – DBMS. Another word for database is *file*, and many authors use the two terms more or less interchangeably. Some, however, prefer to reserve the word database for a collection of linked files. Further confusion may be caused by the fact that in computing the term 'file' is given to any collection of information saved onto disk, e.g. a word processed letter, a computer program, or a spreadsheet. To avoid ambiguity therefore, I use the term 'database' to mean a collection of records, organised into fields or distinct items of information.

These three basic concepts – database, record, and field, are fundamental to all databases – see Figure 1.

## Figure 1. Database concepts

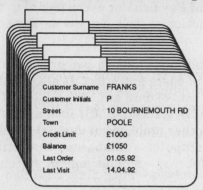

| | |
|---|---|
| Customer Surname | FRANKS |
| Customer Initials | P |
| Street | 10 BOURNEMOUTH RD |
| Town | POOLE |
| Credit Limit | £1000 |
| Balance | £1050 |
| Last Order | 01.05.92 |
| Last Visit | 14.04.92 |

The complete database

Individual record

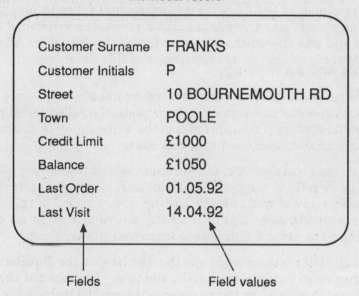

| | |
|---|---|
| Customer Surname | FRANKS |
| Customer Initials | P |
| Street | 10 BOURNEMOUTH RD |
| Town | POOLE |
| Credit Limit | £1000 |
| Balance | £1050 |
| Last Order | 01.05.92 |
| Last Visit | 14.04.92 |

Fields        Field values

## 3. The need for computerised databases

Many businesses still use manual databases for their operations. For example, they have filing cabinets of records for customers, employees and items in stock. A company maintaining a manual database may run into the following typical data management problems:

i.  **Filing order**. The order in which e.g. customer records should be filed may seem straightforward – by numeric customer code or in customer surname order. This works well if all one wants to do is retrieve individual records quickly. But what of more complicated queries or reports – say one wants to find all the customers of a particular type, e.g. living in a particular area, or owing more than a certain amount ? No one filing order could answer both these needs.

ii. **Maintenance**. Perhaps all company employees receive an annual pay rise of five per cent. This will involve amending the Annual Pay field for every record in the personnel database. If any other database holds this information as well, e.g. the salaries database, then this will need updating too.

iii. **Duplication**. If the same information is held on two different databases, as in the above example, it involves duplication of space and effort. It also creates the possibility of inconsistency – perhaps the two sets of data are not updated at the same time, making one set incorrect. Database Management Systems (DBMS) such as dBASE III and IV use complex software to overcome these and other problems of manual databases. They offer not only the ability to store data records on computer – databases – but facilities to maintain and retrieve them in an organised and efficient way – a management system.

## 4. The case study – Quality Wines

All the examples in this book are based around the operations of one company – Quality Wines. Quality Wines is a wholesale wine merchants, it sells a selection of continental wines to clubs, retail off-licenses, restaurants and other organisations.

It buys its wines from a number of British wine importers, and relies on competitive buying and pricing, low stock holdings, and fast turnover to make a profit. It has decided to computerise its present manual system and has chosen the customer file as the first step. All the activities are based around the creation, searching, and maintenance of this database.

# Section 1

# dBASE III – using the Assist

Section 1 is entirely concerned with the menu-driven mode of dBASE III.

dBASE IV users should omit this section and start Section 2, Chapter 3.

## Chapter 1

# Creating and searching a database

**Introduction to the chapter**

*In the first two Chapters you will learn how to perform data management tasks using the Assist – the main menu system that appears when you first enter dBASE III.*

*This is the easiest method for new users, as you can choose the commands that you need from a series of menus.*

*From Section 3 onwards the dot prompt is introduced, which allows you to enter commands directly on the screen.*

## Getting started

dBASE III may be run using an IBM personal computer or compatible, on either a dual floppy disk or hard disk system.

Follow the set of instructions below which applies to your machine.
If you already know how to start up dBASE III then skip to Activity 1

### Dual floppy disk systems

a.   Switch on the computer and place the dBASE system disk 1 in drive A.

b.   The prompt A> or similar will appear in a few seconds.

c.   Type the word dBASE and press the Return or Enter key.
     This large key is to the right of the keyboard and is usually marked with a curled arrow.

d.   In a few seconds you will be prompted to remove system disk 1 and insert system disk 2 into drive A – do this.

e.   Press the Return key again.

f.   Now place the data disk (for the files that you create) on drive B.

g.   The dBASE license screen appears next.

     Now go to Activity 1.

3

### Hard disk systems

a.   Turn on the computer, but do not insert a disk yet.

b.   When you see the prompt C> or C:\> or similar, type the word dBASE and press the Return or Enter key.
     This large key is to the right of the keyboard and is usually marked with a curled arrow.

c.   If this does not work then it is probable that the dBASE III package has been installed in its own directory.
     Do the following:

d.   Type DIR/W after the C> prompt, and press the Return key. The directory for the hard disk is displayed.

e.   Look for a directory with a likely name, e.g. DBASE, or DBASE3.

f.   Change to this directory by typing the letters CD followed by a space and the directory name, e.g. CD DBASE

g.   Press the Return key.

h.   Now type DBASE and press Return again.

     This will run dBASE III – the dBASE license screen appears now.

## Activity 1  *Displaying and using Assist*

### Objectives

1.   To use the dBASE III Assist.

2.   To use the Help system.

3.   To exit from the Assist to dot prompt.

### Introduction

The Assist is your key to the rest of the menu system.
From the menu system you can gain access to data, issue commands, design screens and reports, and many other tasks.
In your first activity you will learn the basic functions of the Assist and how to find your way around it.

### Guided activity

*Entering dBASE III*

1.   On entering dBASE III (see above – Getting Started) the first thing you will see is the license agreement screen. Press the Return key.
     The Assist screen appears – see Figure 1.1.

2.   If the Assist has not appeared, it may be that your computer has been set up differently – see 'Getting Started' above.

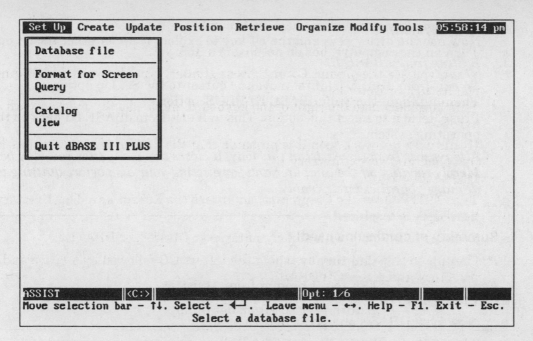

Figure 1.1

If the screen is displaying the dot prompt – a full stop or the word DEMO> or similar, followed by a blinking cursor – press the F2 function key on the keyboard. You will be taken into Assist mode.

You may find that you accidentally end up at the dot prompt in later activities – the F2 key will always take you back to the Assist.

3.  At the top of the screen are 8 pull-down menus. These are the eight major tasks that you can carry out in Assist mode.

    Don't worry if the layout and choices seem rather daunting at first, we will deal with each one as it arises.

4.  At the moment the first menu option – Set Up – is highlighted. Press the right and left arrows and observe how the highlight changes as each menu option is selected. Now use the up and down arrow keys to highlight the choices under a particular option.

## Independent activity

1.  *The Help Option*

    Explore the Help option as follows:

    In the Assist move to the first menu option – Set Up, and make sure that the first option 'Database file' is selected. A brief description of this option appears at the bottom of the screen.

    Press the Function key F1 – the Help key. A Help box appears giving information on this option.

    dBASE III offers context-sensitive help – i.e. it gives you information appropriate to where your cursor or highlight is currently located, or to the stage you have reached.

Press any key to return to the Assist menu.
Now use the arrow keys and the F1 key to explore Help for other Assist options.

2.   *Exiting from dBASE III*

To exit from dBASE III, first move the cursor to the Set Up option.
Then highlight the 'Quit dBASE III PLUS' option.
Press Return to select this option. This will exit from dBASE III back to the operating system

*Always exit from the Assist in this way, it closes down any files you may be using. Merely turning off the computer and / or ejecting your disk before quitting will damage your files irretrievably.*

---

**Summary of commands used**

| | |
|---|---|
| *F1* | Call Help |
| *Esc* | Exit to dot prompt from Assist |
| *F2* | Return to Assist from dot prompt |

---

# Activity 2 *Defining the database structure*

## Objectives

1.   To create a database and define its structure.
2.   To set the date format to British.

## Introduction

As the first computerisation step, Quality Wines are going to create a simple database of its trade customers.

It has the following structure:

| Field 1 Surname | Field 2 Initials | Field 3 Street | Field 4 Town | Field 5 Credit Limit | Field 6 Balance | Field 7 Last Order | Field 8 Last Visit |
|---|---|---|---|---|---|---|---|
| FRANKS | P | 10, BOURNEMOUTH RD | POOLE | 1000 | 1050 | 01/05/92 | 14/04/92 |
| SMITH | JB | WEST DOCKS | SOUTH'N | 750 | 100 | 22/04/91 | 28/05/92 |
| HARRIS | A | 8, WEYMOUTH RD | POOLE | 200 | 3000 | 17/04/92 | 18/05/92 |
| SMITH | P | 7, GOLDEN SQUARE | BOURNEMOUTH | 300 | 000 | 10/12/91 | 12/04/91 |
| ALI | G | 6, CHRISTCHURCH RD | BOURNEMOUTH | 500 | 200 | 07/06/92 | 16/06/92 |
| PATEL | M | 10, KING ST | SOUTHAMPTON | 450 | 300 | 08/02/92 | 20/11/91 |

Figure 1.2

To recap briefly on the database terminology used in the Introduction:

There are 6 customer *records* in the *database* or *file*.
All contain the same *fields* or items of information.
Some fields contain only alphabetic *characters*, others only *numeric* information, and others dates.
The field *values* differ between records e.g. FRANKS, SMITH.

## Guided activity

*Defining the structure of the database*

Planning the database fields – their names, length and type, is the first step of database design.

This has already done for you in Figure 1.2. We can now use dBASE III to define the database structure.

1.   Enter the Assist as you did in Activity 1.

     First move the cursor to the Create menu and make sure that the highlight is on the 'Database file' option.
     The message below the status bar on the screen always explains the meaning of a particular menu choice.
     At the moment it should be reading 'Create a database file structure'
     Press the Return key to execute this choice. (If you make an error and choose the wrong option, the Esc key will always take you back a stage)

2.   ASSIST now prompts you with a list of letters, ABC etc.
     You are being asked which disk drive you wish to create the database on. If your machine has a hard disk, you will save your data on the A drive, i.e. the external floppy disk drive.

3.   If you have not already done do, insert a suitably formatted disk, then make sure that A is highlighted, and press the Return key.
     If you are using a dual floppy disk drive then your dBASE system disk should already be in drive A;
     insert a disk in drive B, move the select highlight to B and press the Return key.

4.   Next you are prompted for the database name. As it is our trade customer database call it TRADCUST (for clarity's sake we will use capital letters throughout for database and field names).
     Database names can consist of up to 8 characters – letters or numbers only with no blanks.

5.   You will now leave the Assist main menu screen and use a screen that allows you to define the database fields. See Figure 1.3.

     The status bar confirms this – it should read:

               [CREATE ][<A:>][   TRADCUST          ][Field: 1/1   ][      ][ ]

Notice the menu of editing commands at the top of the screen. They are self-explanatory with the exception of the ^ symbol which represents the Ctrl key. The flashing cursor shows you where you are up to.

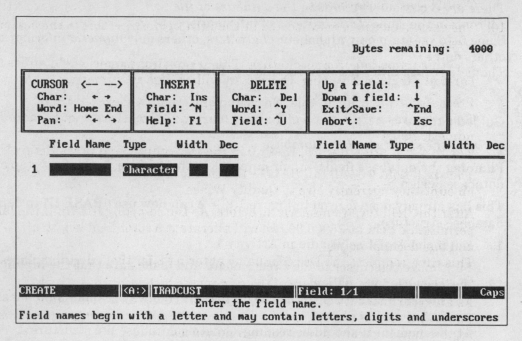

Figure 1.3

6.  The first field name is SURNAME – key this in.

    Notice that it appears in upper case. Press the Return key to move to the next column – Type. SURNAME is a character field, i.e. it consists of letters. Character is the default setting (what you get unless you change it) so merely press Return to confirm this and move to the next column – Width.

    The maximum length of a surname will be 15 characters. Type 15 and press Return again.
    The Next column option – Dec (decimal places) only applies to numeric fields, so you have now defined your first field, and are moved to the next line, ready to define the second field.

7.  The second field is the customer's initials – INITIALS. This is a 2 character field. Define this field in the same way as you did the first.

8.  *Correcting mistakes*

    | | |
    |---|---|
    | The left and right arrow keys | – move a character at a time |
    | Return key | – move forward a field at a time. |
    | Delete key | – delete characters under the cursor or type over unwanted characters |
    | Backspace key | – delete characters to the left of the cursor |
    | Insert key | – insert missing characters (press it again to turn it off when you have finished) |

9. Now define the third field – STREET as 25 characters, and the fourth field – TOWN – as 15 characters.

10. The cursor should be now located at the fifth field name, this is the customer's credit limit – CREDLIM.

    Key this name in and press Return. This is our first numeric field; press the space bar and the default setting, Character, will change to Numeric.

    Press Return to confirm this. No customer's credit will exceed £5000.
    This requires a field width of 4 digits. (currency symbols cannot be stored in numeric fields)
    Key in 4 and press Return. Enter 0 in the Dec column and press Return.

11. The sixth field we will call BALS – the customer's outstanding balance, i.e. the amount they currently owe to Quality Wines.

    Alter the field type to numeric as before. As the company has fixed the largest permissible debt at £5000.00, we will allocate it a total field length of 7 – 6 digits and one decimal point.
    This time complete the Dec column by entering 2 for the 2 decimal places.

12. The seventh field is the date of the customer's last order.
    As an experiment try to enter LAST ORDER DATE as a field name.
    You will find that the spaces are not allowed. Field names must consist of 10 letters, numbers, or less and contain no spaces.
    The underscore character (_) can also be used, but not the dash.

    Alter the field name to LASTORD.
    dBASE III uses a special field type to store dates when your cursor is located on the second column – Type, press the space bar until you see 'Date' appear.

    Press Return to confirm. The field is allocated a standard length of 8. (the format dd/mm/yy = 8 characters)

---

*Note. If you happen to hit the Return key before entering the field name, you may get the message 'input data now Y/N'. Don't worry.*

*The double key press is intended to finish defining fields, and start entering data.*

*Type N, which should take you back to the main menu. Move to the MODIFY option on the menu, and select Database file.*

*You will return to defining the TRADCUST database again.*

---

Two other field types – logical and memo fields – will be dealt with in later Chapters.

13. Now complete the eighth field LASTVIS, which stores the date that the customer was last visited by a company representative.

    Follow the same procedures as for the previous field – LASTORD

14. You have now defined 8 fields, the status bar at the bottom of the screen shows:

    [ CREATE ] [ A:> ] [ TRADCUST ] [ Field 9/9 ]

Press the up and the down arrow keys, and the figure of 9/9 changes as you move between fields.

15. Press the Ctrl and End keys together to save this database structure.
Press the Return key to confirm this, and you will be prompted, 'Input Data Records Now? (Y/N)'.
Enter N and you are returned to the Assist.

16. Notice that the name of the database – TRADCUST – is displayed in the Status Bar at the bottom of the screen.
This indicates that the database is still 'open' or 'active'.

17. *Setting the Date Format.*

Let us now amend the date format if necessary.
dBASE III is an American-produced package, and the US date format is mm/dd/yy – difficult if you are used to the UK format of dd/mm/yy.
Unless it has been reset to UK format permanently when dBASE was installed, you will have to reset it for every new dBASE session.

Press the Esc key to exit to the dot prompt mode. At the prompt type SET DATE BRITISH and press Return. Now press F2 to return to Assist mode.

18. End your dBASE session at this point, – use the Set Up menu to exit as you did in the previous session.

---

**Summary of commands used**

*Ctrl-End*        Pressed together, these 2 keys save a database structure and exit

---

# Activity 3 *Entering data into the database*

## Objectives

1. To enter six records into the TRADCUST database.
2. To amend database records.

## Introduction

At the moment we have an empty database – a structure with no contents.
We will be adding records for some of Quality Wines trade customers.
If you are starting a new dBASE session then you will have to set the date format to British as above; once you quit dBASE the date reverts to US format.

 **Guided activity**

*From now on I shall be assuming that you have mastered the two basic steps of selecting a menu choice – i.e. Use the arrow key to highlight the choice, Press the Return key to select.*
*I will be using the word 'select' to refer to these two steps in future activities.*

1.  Retrieve the TRADCUST database first.

    Highlight the Main Menu choice 'Set Up', and press the Return key to take the 'Database File' option.

2.  Select the correct drive and database.
    Answer N to the prompt 'Is the File indexed? (Y/N)'
    'TRADCUST' appears in the status bar.

3.  Highlight the main Menu choice 'Update' and select the Append option. (Append means to add records to the end of a file)
    A template is displayed, showing the fields that you have defined – see Figure 1.4.

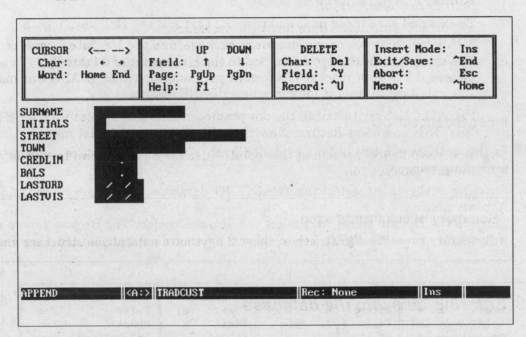

Figure 1.4

The fields and field widths for the TRADCUST database are shown as blank areas next to the field names.
Notice the Editing Keys listed at the top of the screen. The ^ symbol represents the Ctrl key.

4.  Enter the 6 customer records shown in figure 1.2 *using capital letters*. (use the Caps Lock key)

    Enter the data exactly as shown, it will be important in our later activities.

5.  Notes:

    ❐   If you make a mistake use the arrow keys and overtype. The Delete, Backspace and Insert keys can also be used.
        If the data that you enter completely fills the field, then the cursor will automatically advance to the next field. Otherwise you must press the Return key.

❏ Be careful to distinguish the digit 1 from the capital letter I, and the digit 0 from capital O.

❏ Enter the date in the UK format discussed above, dBASE will prevent you from entering an invalid date.

6. When you have completed the last field of the first record, the template will become blank again, ready for the next record.
If you need to return to a previous record use the PgUp key.
The PgDn key moves you forward in the database.
When you have finished entering the records, the status bar will confirm the number of records in the database – 6.

7. To exit and save these records Press the Ctrl and the End keys together. You will exit to the Assist.

8. The status bar at the bottom of the screen confirms that TRADCUST is still open for use.

### Independent activity

In this activity you will learn a central database maintenance tasks – editing or amending records.

Starting at the Assist, select the TRADCUST database, if necessary (see Guided Activity above).
Move to the Update menu, and select the 'Browse' option. The Browse screen appears; if necessary press the Pg Up key to show the 6 records already added – see Figure 1.5

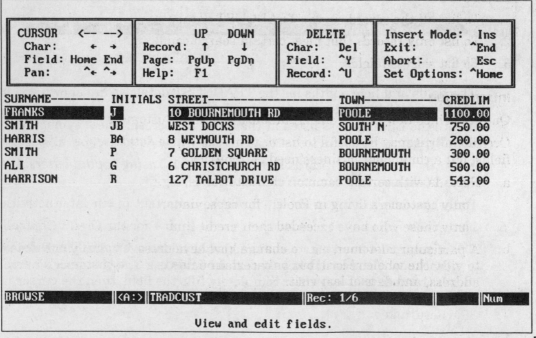

| CURSOR | <-- --> | | UP | DOWN | DELETE | | Insert Mode: | Ins |
|---|---|---|---|---|---|---|---|---|
| Char: | ← → | Record: | ↑ | ↓ | Char: | Del | Exit: | ^End |
| Field: Home End | | Page: | PgUp | PgDn | Field: | ^Y | Abort: | Esc |
| Pan: | ^← ^→ | Help: | F1 | | Record: | ^U | Set Options: | ^Home |

| SURNAME——— | INITIALS | STREET————————— | TOWN———— | CREDLIM |
|---|---|---|---|---|
| FRANKS | J | 10 BOURNEMOUTH RD | POOLE | 1100.00 |
| SMITH | JB | WEST DOCKS | SOUTH'N | 750.00 |
| HARRIS | BA | 8 WEYMOUTH RD | POOLE | 200.00 |
| SMITH | P | 7 GOLDEN SQUARE | BOURNEMOUTH | 300.00 |
| ALI | G | 6 CHRISTCHURCH RD | BOURNEMOUTH | 500.00 |
| HARRISON | R | 127 TALBOT DRIVE | POOLE | 543.00 |

| BROWSE | | <A:> TRADCUST | | Rec: 1/6 | | | Num |

View and edit fields.

Figure 1.5

Now carry out the following amendments, using the editing keys shown below – you may need to scroll right and left to edit all the fields:

a.   Amend the last visit for HARRIS to 20/06/92

b.   Alter FRANKS's credit limit to 1100.

c.   Alter the last order date for ALI to 08/07/92

Exit and save as before,and exit dBASE.

---

**Summary of commands used**

In the BROWSE Screen:

| | |
|---|---|
| *Return and arrow keys* | Move between fields |
| *PgUp and PgDn keys* | Move between records |
| *Ctrl-Right Arrow* | Scroll Right |
| *Ctrl-Left Arrow* | Scroll Left |
| *Delete and backspace keys* | Delete data |
| *Insert key* | Insert data |
| *Ctrl and End keys together* | Exit and save database |

---

# Activity 4 *Retrieving information from the database*

### Objectives

1.   To list all the records in the TRADCUST database.

2.   To list only records that meet certain search conditions.

3.   To list selected fields.

### Introduction

Quality Wines now have a small database of Trade Customers.

Occasionally it may be useful to list or print the whole database, i.e. all customers, all fields, but a commoner business need is to retrieve:

a.   Records with certain common characteristics, e.g.

only customers living in Poole – for reps. visits;

only those who have exceeded their credit limit – for the Credit Controller.

b.   A particular customer, e.g. to change his/her address. Typically one does not need to view the whole record, but only certain fields, e.g. the customer's name, address, and date of last visit.

**Guided activity**

1. Make sure the TRADCUST database is open first – see Activity 3.
   Move to the Main Menu option 'Retrieve' and select the LIST option,
   Select the sub-option 'Execute the command '.

2. Reply N to the question,' Direct the output to the Printer? [Y/N] '.
   All the fields of the records that you have created should now be displayed on
   screen – if not, repeat the above steps.

3. Check the 6 customer records are correct.
   You will see that a blank record may have been appended to the end of the
   database. This will accommodate the next record to be added.
   Notice also that the fields are not particularly well displayed. The LIST command
   merely lists every field of every record to printer or screen.
   We will be formatting the screen and creating more attractive reports later.

4. Retrieving selected records involves specifying a search condition, e.g. surname =
   'SMITH'.
   There are several stages to this, which involve some fairly complex menu choices
   – remember :

   ❒ Use the arrow keys to move to a particular menu choice
   ❒ Use the Return key to select a particular menu choice
   ❒ The ESC key will always take you back a menu stage
   ❒ The command display at the bottom of the screen shows the stage you have
      reached.

   Return to the main menu by pressing the ESC Key.

5. Let's retrieve the two records for the two customers whose surname is Smith.
   First select DISPLAY from the RETRIEVE menu. Select SPECIFY SCOPE from
   the sub-menu that appears.
   Then choose ALL – to tell dBase III you want to search all the records in the
   database.

   Your screen will look like Figure 1.6

6. Next press the down arrow key to take you into the option BUILD A SEARCH
   CONDITION. Select this.
   Now select SURNAME from the field list that appears. (Remember we are
   searching on the surname field for all customers called SMITH)

7. Select the = (Equal to) operator from the list displayed.
   Enter SMITH (in capital letters) in the prompt box that appears.

8. Now select the NO MORE CONDITIONS, option, followed by the EXECUTE
   THE COMMAND option.
   The database of customers is searched and the two records for Smith are
   retrieved.
   Notice that all the fields appear on screen. If not you will need to re-input the
   search statement, using steps 5 – 8 above.

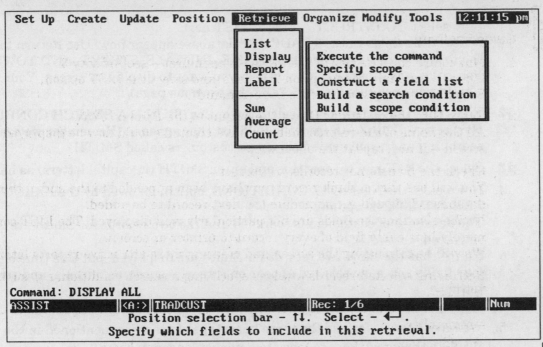

Figure 1.6

9. Now let's repeat our search for customers surnamed Smith, but this time make the display more readable by displaying the customer's name and address only.

10. Select DISPLAY from the RETRIEVE menu.
Select SPECIFY SCOPE from the sub-menu. Then select ALL.

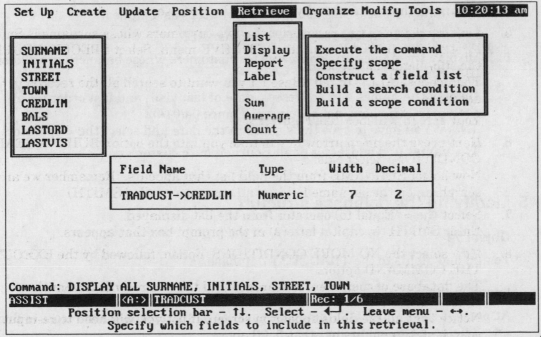

Figure 1.7

15

11. Now select CONSTRUCT A FIELD LIST next.
    A list of the fields in the TRADCUST database appear now. Use Return to select the first 4 fields in the list – SURNAME, INITIALS, STREET, AND TOWN.
    You have now selected the fields that you want to display on screen. Your screen should now look like Figure 1.7 (on the previous page).

12. Press the right arrow key to select the option, 'BUILD A SEARCH CONDITION'
    Now select SURNAME from the field list that appears. (Remember we are searching on the surname field for all customers called SMITH)

13. Select the = (Equal to) operator and enter SMITH (in capital letters) as before.

14. Now select the NO MORE CONDITIONS, option, followed by the EXECUTE THE COMMAND option.
    The database of customers is searched and the two records for Smith are retrieved.
    Notice that the same two records for Smith are displayed, but this time only the four fields you have selected appear on screen. – surname, initials, and street and town.
    If not you will need to re-input the search statement.

15. We have now performed the three basic type of searches mentioned in the Introduction:

    Retrieving all fields of all records (steps 1 – 4)
    Retrieving all fields of selected records (steps 5 – 8)
    Retrieving selected fields of selected records (steps 9 – 14)

### Independent exercises

Build the following searches using the above steps as a guide:

a. Display the complete record for customer ALI.

b. Display the names and addresses for customers whose balances are 200 or more. (BALS > 200)

c. Display the names and addresses, date of last visit, and last order for all customers who have not been visited since 04/01/92.
   (Note: You have to type the slashes in the date and select the < operator)

d. The names and addresses of all Bournemouth customers.

## Activity 5 Modifying the database structure

### Objective

To add new fields to the TRADCUST database.

### Introduction

At present the TRADCUST database consists of six records. Each record is divided into 8 fields, SURNAME, INITIALS, etc.

We are going to modify this structure by adding new fields.

**Guided activity**

1.  If you are starting a new dBASE session move to the Set Up menu and select the TRADCUST database.
    Move to the menu option 'Modify' and select 'Database file'.
    The present fields in the database are displayed – see Figure 1.8.

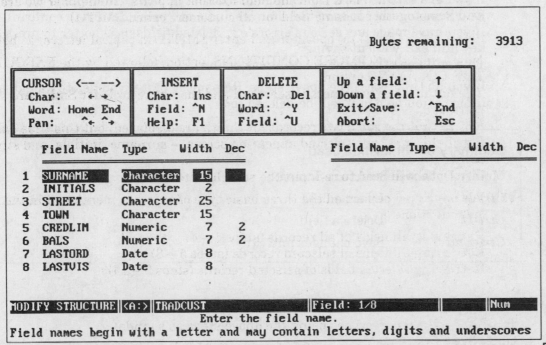

```
                                            Bytes remaining:    3913

┌─────────────────┬──────────────┬───────────────┬──────────────────────┐
│ CURSOR  <-- -->  │   INSERT     │    DELETE     │ Up a field:     ↑    │
│ Char:    ← →     │ Char:  Ins   │ Char:   Del   │ Down a field:   ↓    │
│ Word: Home End   │ Field: ^N    │ Word:   ^Y    │ Exit/Save:     ^End  │
│ Pan:    ^← ^→    │ Help:  F1    │ Field:  ^U    │ Abort:         Esc   │
└─────────────────┴──────────────┴───────────────┴──────────────────────┘

    Field Name   Type    Width Dec        Field Name   Type    Width Dec

 1  SURNAME      Character  15
 2  INITIALS     Character   2
 3  STREET       Character  25
 4  TOWN         Character  15
 5  CREDLIM      Numeric     7    2
 6  BALS         Numeric     7    2
 7  LASTORD      Date        8
 8  LASTVIS      Date        8


┌MODIFY STRUCTURE┬<A:>┬TRADCUST──────────────┬Field: 1/8───────┬───Num─┐
                  Enter the field name.
Field names begin with a letter and may contain letters, digits and underscores
```

Figure 1.8

2.  We are going to insert a field to hold the customer's reference number.
    Highlight the SURNAME field and press the Ctrl and N keys together.
    A blank field appears above the surname field.
    Name this field CUSTREF and define it as a character field, length 4 characters.

3.  We will now create a second new field which will indicate if a customer gets extended credit facilities or not.
    All we wish to store is a single character, Y for yes, or N for no.
    Highlight the LASTORD field, and press Ctrl-N again. A blank field appears.
    Type in the field name EXCREDIT and press Return.
    Now press the Space Bar to change the field type to logical, and press Return to confirm.
    A logical field is always one character long and can hold the values T for true or F for false, or, if preferred, Y for yes or N for no.

4.  Next use the down arrow to move past the last field.
    In the blank space provided, create a new field NOTES, to hold notes about each customer.

17

Define this field as a memo field; it is automatically allocated a width of 10 characters, but allows you to store up to 512k of notes about each customer record in a related record.

5. Press the down arrow again and room for a 12th field is added.
To delete this unwanted field, make sure that it is highlighted and press the Ctrl and U keys together.

6. If you are satisfied that the changed structure is correct then press the Ctrl and End keys together to save the changes and exit. (press Return to confirm)
If you have made any serious errors e.g. deleted fields, it is better to press the Esc key and exit without saving.
This will keep the database as it was before.

If you do this repeat the above steps. Remember that if you delete a field, any information held in it will be deleted too.

---

**Summary of commands used**

Modify Database Structure Screen:

| | |
|---|---|
| *Ctrl-N* | Insert a field |
| *Ctrl-U* | Delete a field |
| *Ctrl-End* | Save changes and exit |

---

# Activity 6 Adding records to the database

### Objective

To add new records to the TRADCUST database.

### Introduction

At the moment the TRADCUST database contains only six records.
We shall be increasing this number to about 20, and also entering information in the new fields that we have created in the previous activity.

### Guided activity

1. If you are starting a new dBASE session make sure that the TRADCUST database is open for use, and that you have SET DATE BRITISH – see Activity 3.

2. Move to the Update menu, and select Browse.
You will see that there is only room to display the first 5 fields or so across the screen. Press Esc.

3. Now select Edit from the Update menu.
Unlike Browse, the Edit command displays a single record at a time.

Check the status bar at the bottom of the screen – if it displays '1/6' then the first record for customer FRANKS should be displayed. If not, use the Pg Up key until you reach the first record.

4.   Notice that the 3 new fields, CUSTREF, EXCREDIT, and NOTES are currently blank. Complete these fields as follows:

Remember to use the Caps Lock key so all the new information is entered in upper case.

CUSTREF – enter the reference number T001 for FRANKS, T002 for SMITH JB, etc. (use the numeric digit 0, not the letter O)

EXCREDIT – enter Y in this field for FRANKS and HARRIS, N for the other 4 customers.

5.   *Completing Memo fields.*

Memo fields allow us to attach blocks of information to a record that would be inconvenient in a fixed length field.
We are going to use it to store notes on a few of the customers.

6.   Highlight the NOTES field for the first record – FRANKS – and press the Ctrl and Home keys together.

A word processing screen appears. Type the following notes:

1.   Do not send monthly statement.

2.   Always obtain owner's personal signature for  deliveries.

Press the Ctrl and End Keys together, the text is saved, and you are returned to the Edit screen.
Use the same operations if you want to amend a memo field.
Now press the Ctrl and End keys together to save the changes, and return to Assist.

7.   *Adding Records*

---

*If you are using the special educational 'restricted' version of DBASE III, remember that the maximum number of records per database is 32, after this the database becomes unusable.*

*If you are using this version then the dot prompt may display 'demo>' instead of a single dot.*

---

Move to the Update menu and select the Append option. Now add at least 10 more records to the TRADCUST database.
For the TOWN field use BOURNEMOUTH, SOUTHAMPTON, RINGWOOD, WEYMOUTH and one record for DORCHESTER.

Supply the rest of the details yourself, but make sure that:
a. There are two J WILSON's both in the town WEYMOUTH.
b. Some of the dates in the LASTORD field are more than a year old.
This information will be used in later searches of the database.

Remember that:

❏   you can use the up and down arrow keys to move between fields;

❏   Pg Up and Pg Dn to move between records.

8.   When you have finished appending records, exit to Assist using Ctrl-End.

---

**Summary of commands used**

From the Update Menu:

*Append*            Add a new record to the end of the database

*Browse*            Edits records using a full-screen display

*Edit*              Display an individual record for editing

From Append, Browse or Edit Options:

*Ctrl-Home*         When cursor is located on a memo field, opens it for editing

---

# Activity 7 Deleting records from the database

## Objectives
1.   To mark individual records for deletion.
2.   To mark selected records for deletion.
3.   To recall records marked for deletion.
4.   To remove records marked for deletion permanently.

## Introduction
Part of routine database maintenance is the removal of records that, for one reason or another, are no longer required.

One may need to remove an individual record e.g. Customer SMITH, or select all records in a particular category for deletion, e.g. customers who have not placed orders for over a year.

In dBASE III the procedure is very similar to that for listing or displaying records used in Activity 4.

One builds a search condition to delete records meeting certain conditions.

## Guided activity

1.   If you are starting a new dBASE session, make sure that the TRADCUST database is open, and date is set to UK format.
     We are going to mark for deletion the records of customers who have not placed an order for a year or over.
     Select the Delete option from the Update menu.
2.   Select the option 'Build a Search Condition' first.
     Then select the LASTORD field from the list that appears – see Figure 1.9.

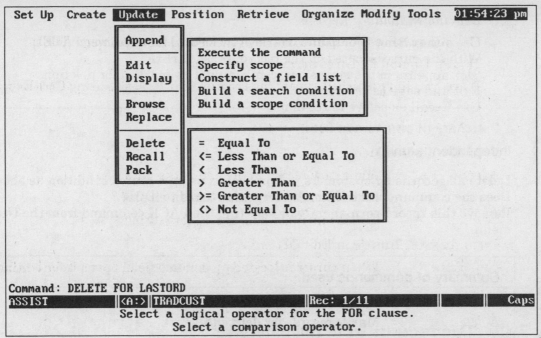

Figure 1.9

Select the '< Less Than' operator from the list. The LASTORD field must be less than the date a year ago. (Note: 'less than' in numeric terms means over a year ago) Type the date of a year ago, remembering to insert the slashes.

Then select the option 'No more conditions' followed by, 'Execute the command'.

3.  After you execute this command you will get the message '...... Records deleted'. If you get the message 'No records deleted', you will need to browse the database and amend the LASTORD field of a few records to dates matching the condition – more than a year ago. Then repeat the above steps.

4.  Take the BROWSE option and scroll through the records one by one.
    You may be puzzled that no records have actually disappeared from the database. This is because the DELETE command only marks records for deletion, as the status bar will indicate.
    Scroll the records again, looking at the status bar. Confirm that the correct records have been marked 'Del' in the status bar.
    You may need to scroll the LASTORD field into view by pressing the Ctrl key, together with the right arrow keys.
    Exit from Browse to Assist.

5.  *Recalling Marked Records*

    Select Recall from the Update menu. Select the' Specify scope' option as All. Then take the option 'Execute the command'.
    This will unmark the deleted records. A message confirms this.

6.  Confirm the records have been recalled by browsing the database again, and making sure that 'Del' has disappeared from the status bar.

7.  *Deleting Individual Records*

    Use either Browse or Edit to retrieve the record for customer PATEL.
    With the cursor located on the record, press Ctrl-U.
    'Del' appears in the status bar, confirming it as marked for deletion.
    Exit and save as before.
    Use Recall as before to recall it.

### Independent activity

Delete all records for customers in Dorchester, using a search condition as above.
Does the command work if Dorchester is shortened to 'DOR'?
Remove this record permanently by selecting the PACK command from the Update menu.

---

**Summary of commands used.**

From the Update Menu:

| | |
|---|---|
| *Delete* | Marks records for deletion |
| *Recall* | Unmarks deleted records |
| *Pack* | Permanently removes deleted records |

In Browse or Edit Mode

| | |
|---|---|
| *CTRL-U* | Marks/Unmarks a record for deletion |

---

# Activity 8 *Arithmetic operations – count, sum and average*

### Objectives

1.  To count all the records in a database, or records meeting certain conditions.
2.  To find the total of numeric fields.
3.  To find the average of numeric fields.

### Introduction

Dbase III provides a limited number of mathematical operations that allow one to manipulate data held in mathematical fields

### Guided activities

If you are starting a new dBASE session, ensure that the TRADCUST database is opened for use.

1.  Move to the Retrieve menu and select Count.
    Select 'Execute the command' next. How many records are in the database?

2. Now select Average from the Retrieve menu, followed by 'Execute the Command'. What do the totals produced mean?

3. Select Sum from the Retrieve menu, followed by 'Execute the Command'. What do the totals produced mean?

4. We can also use these three commands with conditions.

   Select Count, then 'Build a search condition'.
   Select TOWN from the list of fields that appears.
   Select '= Equal to' from the list of operators.
   Enter POOLE in upper case.
   Select' No more conditions' then' Execute the command'
   The number of Poole customers are displayed.

5. Now let's find out the total owed by Weymouth customers.
   Select Sum, followed by 'Construct a field list'. Select BALS from the field list.
   Press the Right arrow key and select 'Build a search condition'.
   Select TOWN from the list of fields.
   Select '= Equal to' from the list of operators.
   Enter weymouth in lower case.
   Select 'No more conditions' then 'Execute the command'
   You will get a message, 'No records summed'.
   For search conditions, the case of the letters that you enter must match the case of the fields in the database.

## Independent exercises

Find the average balance for all customers.

Find the average credit rating for all Southampton customers.

Find the total owed by all Bournemouth customers.

Count the number of Bournemouth customers.

---

**Summary of commands used**

Under the Retrieve Menu.

| | |
|---|---|
| *Count* | Counts the number of records |
| *Sum* | Totals numeric fields |
| *Average* | Finds the average of numeric fields |

---

# Activity 9 *Indexing the database*

## Objectives

1. To create indexes for the TRADCUST database.

2. To display records in indexed sequence.

### Introduction

A common business need is to present the same information in a variety of orders, e.g. a list of customers either in name or town order.

At the moment our database is in serial or unordered sequence – i.e. the records are in no particular order. This makes it difficult to search once it gets over a certain length. First we are going to index the database on the TOWN field, so, for example, all the Bournemouth customers will be grouped together, followed by all the Dorchester customers and so on.

The field that is used to organise a file into a particular sequence is called the key field or record key.

As we will see later it is possible to index a file on more than one key, e.g. surname order within town. Town would then be the primary key, and surname the secondary key.

Then in Activity 11 we will look briefly at the second major method of reorganising database records – sorting.

Sorting works by physically rearranging the records and storing them in a second database, leaving the original database unchanged. Indexing works by creating an index file containing the pointers to database records.

This has the advantage of economising on disk space – only a small index file is needed to access the database in a new sequence.

Sorting records into a new database gives faster access to them than using an index (this is not noticeable in the small databases we are creating) at the price of duplicating the information over two databases.

But if one database is changed then the other needs updating too if it is not to become inconsistent with the first.

With indexing however, any indexes can be automatically updated whenever records are changed or added.

### Guided activity

1. If you are starting a new dBASE session, make sure that the TRADCUST database is open, and that the date format is set to UK.

   Move to the Organise menu and select the Index option. A Prompt box appears next, asking you to' Enter an index key expression' – see Figure 1.10.

   Our first index will place the records in surname order, so enter the field name SURNAME.

2. You are then prompted for the drive letter.
   Your index file should be on the same disk and drive as the database it indexes – TRADCUST.
   Select the appropriate letter.

3. You are now prompted for the name of the file – enter CUSNAME and press Return.
   A message is now displayed '100% indexed'. The index is now stored as a separate file – CUSNAME with the extension.NDX.

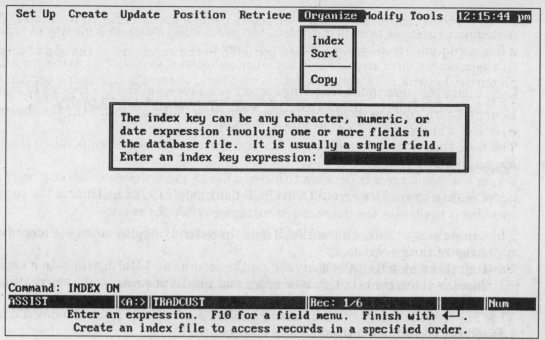

```
Set Up  Create  Update  Position  Retrieve  Organize Modify Tools  12:15:44 pm
                                       Index
                                       Sort

                                       Copy

           The index key can be any character, numeric, or
           date expression involving one or more fields in
           the database file.  It is usually a single field.
           Enter an index key expression: ▮

Command: INDEX ON
ASSIST            <A:> TRADCUST              Rec: 1/6              Num
           Enter an expression.  F10 for a field menu.  Finish with ←.
           Create an index file to access records in a specified order.
```

Figure 1.10

4.    You are now returned to Assist.
      Select Browse from the Update menu – the records are now displayed in customer
      surname order.
      Press Esc to return to Assist.
      Select Edit from the Update menu – the records are displayed a record at a time
      in surname order.
      Notice that the current record numbers appearing in the status bar are no longer
      in numeric sequence.
      This is because the records remain in the same physical sequence in the database,
      but are now displayed in a new order using the index that we have just created.

5.    *Indexing on more than one field*

      We are going to create a list of customers in surname order within town.
      This involves creating an index based on two key fields. i.e. TOWN is the primary
      key field, within which the records are ordered by SURNAME, the secondary key.
      Repeat steps 1 – 4 above, but this time enter TOWN+SURNAME as the index
      expression, and call the index file NAMETOWN.
      If you press F10 then you can select the fields from a field list.

6.    *Combining fields of different data types*

      It is possible to create an index using character, numeric or date fields. (but not
      memo or logical fields). Sometimes we want to combine different field types as an
      index expression, e.g. index the customer records by the date of their last visit,
      within town.
      TOWN the primary key is alphabetic, but LASTVIS the secondary key is a date
      field.

25

We must convert the date to characters using a special dBASE function DTOC (date to character).
A number of these functions are included in the summary at the end of this activity.

7. Create this new index following steps 1 – 4 above, calling the index VISTOWN. Under the Index expression option enter, TOWN+DTOC(LASTVIS)
Now display the records in this new order.

## Independent activities

1. Create a new index on the CUSTREF field, call it CUSTREF.
Use it to display the database in customer reference order.

2. Create a new index on the BALS field, in order to display customer records in order of their balance.
Call this index BALANCE.
Display the records in this new order and return to Assist.

---

**Summary of functions used**

| | |
|---|---|
| *STR(<FIELDNAME>)  e.g. STR(CREDLIM)* | converts numeric fields to character fields |
| *DTOC(FIELDNAME)* | converts date fields to character fields |
| *UPPER(FIELDNAME)* | converts lower to uppercase letters for indexing purposes |

---

# Activity 10 *Activating and deleting indexes*

### Objectives

1. To call up and use an existing index.
2. To delete an unwanted index.

### Introduction

Now that we have created several indexes to the TRADCUST database we need to know how to use and maintain them.
The following activities cover using and deleting indexes

### Guided activity

1. To activate an existing index.
If you are continuing from Activity 9, the TRADCUST database is still indexed in order of customer balance using the BALANCE index – the last index created.
It is useful to be able to redisplay it in a new order.

2.   Move to the Set Up menu and select 'Database file'.
     Select TRADCUST. Answer Y to the prompt, 'Is the file indexed [Y/N]?'

3.   Select the NAMETOWN and VISTOWN indexes from the list displayed.

4.   Press the right arrow key and select Browse to browse the database.
     Select the customer record for SMITH JB, and amend the name of the town from
     SOUTH'N to SOUTHAMPTON.

     Press Ctrl-End to exit and save.
     As the TOWN field is a key field, the indexes will be re-organised automatically –
     provided that they have been opened first as we have done.

     Warning:
     If you intend to amend a database make sure that any idexes that could be
     affected are opened, otherwise when the index is next used it will be unable to
     locate the amended record and an error message may be displayed.

5.   *Deleting an index*
     Move to the Tools menu and select the Erase option. Select the appropriate drive,
     and a list of all files appears.
     Select VISTOWN.NDX and press Return.
     A message confirms 'File has been deleted'
     Any file can be deleted in this way, but care must be taken not to erase the wrong
     file!

# Activity 11  *Sorting the database*

### Objective

To sort the TRADCUST database into a new order.

### Introduction

On occasions it may be useful to produce a copy of a database, sorted into a new order
– although this means having to maintain two separate databases – see Activity 10,
Introduction.
We are going to create a copy of TRADCUST, sorted by customer reference within
town.
As customer references, names and addresses do not change frequently, this could be
useful, when printed out, for cross-referencing customer names and reference
numbers.

### Guided activity

1.   Starting from Assist, make sure that the TRADCUST database is open for use.

2.   Move to the Organise menu and select the option, 'Sort'.

3. A list of possible sort fields is displayed. (the field NOTES is a memo field, and cannot be used to sort)
   We are going to create a new database sorted on customer reference within town. Highlight TOWN, the primary sort field.
   The field name will now appear in a window, as in Figure 1.11.

   Press Return.

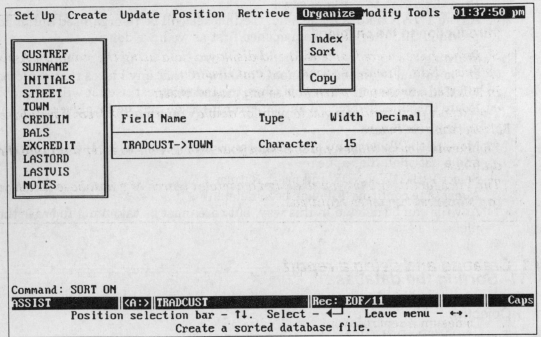

Figure 1.11

4. Now repeat the above operations for our secondary sort field CUSTREF.
   Next press the Right Arrow key and select the appropriate drive for the sorted version of the database.

5. You will be prompted for a file name, call the new database CUSTREF.

6. The sort now takes place.
   Use the Set Up menu to retrieve this new database.
   Check that the records are sorted correctly, i.e. customer reference within town.

## Independent activity

The CUSTREF database only needs the fields CUSTREF, SURNAME, STREET, TOWN. Delete the other fields as follows:

1. Make sure that the database is open – check the status bar.

2. Move to the Modify Menu, and select 'Database file'

3. When the Modify Structure screen appears, delete the unwanted fields.

4. Exit and save, then use List to check the records.

# Chapter 2

# Producing reports, screens and views

---

### Introduction to the chapter

*So far we have entered, amended and displayed data using the standard Assist options – Edit, Browse, Append, List and Display.*

*In this Chapter we will learn how to improve on these:*

*The Report facility allows you to print or display information from a database in a clear, readable report.*

*The Forms facility allows you to design your own screens to enter data into the database.*

*The View facility allows you to design a complex search of a database which you can store and run when required.*

---

## Activity 1 *Creating and using a report*

### Objectives

1.   To design a report layout.
2.   To save the report for future use.
3.   To print or display the report.
4.   To modify the report.

### Introduction

We have learnt how to retrieve and display records in a number of ways.
The format of such standard displays, however, becomes crowded and unattractive once more than a few fields are displayed.
An important advantage of database management systems such as dBASE is their ability to produce clear, well laid-out reports, based on information stored in a database.

We are going to produce a report on the credit status of Quality Wines trade customers – see Figure 2.1

 **Guided activities**

1.   To design a report you must first select the database that the report is based on. If you want the records displayed in a particular order, then the correct index must be open too.

```
                          Customer Credit Report

        Customer   Customer Name      Customer  Over Limit (-)
        Reference                     Balance

        T004       SMITH         P        0.00        300.00
        T007       MUIR          J        0.00          0.00
        T005       ALI           G      200.00        300.00
        T009       HOOD          RL     234.00         66.00
        T011       HARRISON      R      567.00        -24.00
        T006       PATEL         M      900.00       -350.00
        T012       ROGERSON      H      900.00        100.00
        T002       SMITH         JB    2664.00      -1914.00
        T001       FRANKS        J     3050.00      -1950.00
        T010       CARPENTER     S     4050.00        -50.00
        T003       HARRIS        BA    5244.64      -5044.64
        *** Total ***
                                      17809.64      -8566.64
```

Figure 2.1

2.  First move to the Set Up menu and select 'Database file'.
    Select the appropriate drive for TRADCUST, then select TRADCUST itself.
    Select the index file BALANCE.NDX which places customers in order of their balance.

3.  Use the Right Arrow key to move to the Create menu and select the Report option.
    Select the appropriate drive – the report should be on the same drive as TRADCUST on which it is based.
    Name the report CREDREP and press Return.

4.  The Report Design Screen appears now – see Figure 2.2

    There are 5 main menu options: Options, Groups, Columns, Locate, and Exit.

5.  Use the Right and Left arrow keys to move across the menus – Each menu offers its own options when highlighted.

    The Up and Down arrow keys move up and down these options.
    Notice the list of editing keys at the bottom of the screen. This can be turned on and off by pressing the F1 key.

    *Select an option in the usual way – by highlighting it and then pressing Return.*

    *If you make a mistake in the following activities, then the Esc key will always take you back a stage.*

    *Pressed more than once it offers you the option to abort the operation and start again.*

6.  *Page Title*
    First move to the Options menu – this menu defines the page title, page settings, and print requirements.
    Select 'Page title'.

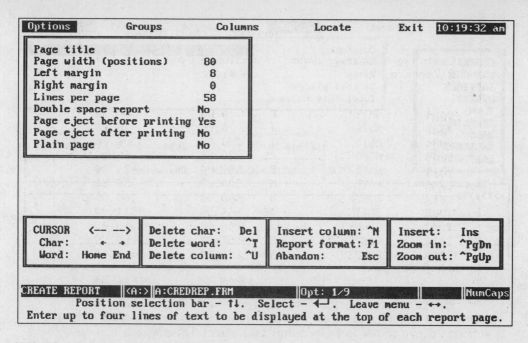

Figure 2.2

7.    An arrowhead appears in the data entry area and a box opens up, allowing you to enter up to 4 lines of page title.
Type the title 'Customer Credit Report' and press Return.
Press Ctrl-End to finish the title.

8.    If you have access to a printer, then use the Options menu to alter the following settings – they work with most printers.
Select 'Page eject after printing'.
Press Return to change the setting to 'YES'.
Repeat for the setting 'Double space report'.

9.    *The main body of the report*

Press the Right Arrow key to move to the Columns menu.
Each column will hold a field from the TRADCUST database, or the result of a calculation, e.g. subtracting one field from another.

10.   Select the Contents option first.
Press F10 to display a list of field names – see Figure 2.3.

The first column will contain the customer reference – select CUSTREF from the field list – it is moved to the Contents box.
Press Return again to 'deselect' the Contents option.

11.   Now select the Heading option – this will contain the column heading.

Type in the word 'Customer' and press Return. Type the word 'Reference' on the next heading line and press Return again.
Now press Ctrl-End to complete the first column.

12.   Notice that a report template is being drawn below, showing the first column that you have defined.
It contains the field CUSTREF (shown as XXXX) and, a two line column heading – 'Customer Reference '

31

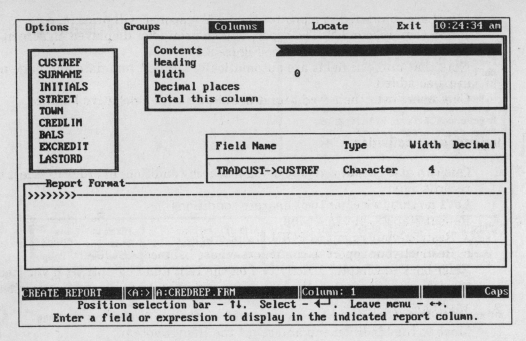

Figure 2.3

13. Press the Pg Dn key to begin column 2.
    Select the Contents option again, but this time type
    SURNAME+INITIALS to join these two fields.
    Press Return.

14. Now select the Heading option.
    Call the heading 'Customer Name' (on one line)
    Press Ctrl-End to finish designing the second column.

15 Press Pg Dn to start the third column.
    Repeat steps 10-12 above.
    The column contents are the BALS field.
    The column heading is two lines – 'Customer Balance'

16. Our fourth and final column shows the difference between the customer's balance
    and their credit limit. Customers over their limit will have a negative balance.
    The column contents are CREDLIM-BALS
    The column heading is 'Over Limit (-)'.

17. Finally use the Right Arrow key to move to the Exit menu.
    Select Save and the report file is saved to disk.
    You are returned to Assist.
    If you get an error message you will need to return and modify your report.
    A common error is the width of the column headings exceeding the paper or
    screen size.
    Putting long column headings on two lines as we have done helps to avoid this.

18. *Displaying / Printing the report*
    In Assist, move to the Retrieve menu, and select the Report option.
    Select the appropriate drive, and then the report CREDREP.FRM.
    Select 'Execute the command'.

If you are connected to a printer then a Y response will print it.
If not, then respond N. The report will be printed or displayed on screen in ascending order of balance. (see Figure 2.1)
Note that numeric fields are automatically totalled, and date and page numbering are also added.
Customers over their credit limit are shown with a negative balance.

## Independent activities

1.  One can also output a report using a search condition, in order to select certain records only.
    Let's do this twice, for two separate conditions.
    Repeat step 18, but this time:
    a. Restrict your report to POOLE customers.
    b. Restrict your report to customers whose balance > £2000
    Refer back to Chapter 1 Activity 4 on the Edit and List options if you need to refresh your memory on the steps involved in building a search condition.

2.  *Modifying a report*

    Move to the Modify menu and select the Report option.

    Select CREDREP.

    When the Report Design Screen appears, make the following modifications:

    a.  Give the page title a second line:
        'Showing Customers Above Credit Limit'

    b.  Move to the Columns menu and press Pg Dn until the BALS column appears.

    c.  Press Ctrl-N and a new column is inserted – it is shown as a '?' on the template.

    d.  Make the Contents CREDLIM
        Make the Heading 'Credit Limit'

    e.  Save the report and run it again – the new column will be displayed.

---

### Summary of commands used

At Assist

| | |
|---|---|
| *Report option from the Create menu* | Create a new report |
| *Report option from the Modify menu* | Modify a report |
| *Report option from the Retrieve option* | Print/Display a report |

On Report Design Screen

| | |
|---|---|
| *F1* | Display Editing options |
| *F10* | Display field list |
| *Ctrl-End* | Finish defining a column |

---

| Ctrl-N | Insert a new column |
|--------|---------------------|
| Ctrl-U | Delete a column |
| Pg Dn | Move to next column |

## Activity 2 *Creating and using a screen format*

### Objectives

1. To create a data entry screen.
2. To use the screen to add and amend records.

### Introduction

So far we have used the standard dBASE III screen formats for data entry and display – e.g. the Edit screen which displays individual records, and the Browse screen which displays records a screenful at a time.

However Edit and Browse may cause problems for inexperienced users – records may be accidentally changed or deleted, because there is no control over how the data is to be entered.

You have seen in the previous activity that a special report form can improve the appearance of printed reports. Similarly, designing your own screen format can improve on the standard dBASE III data entry screens.

Like a report, a format is based upon a database. Unlike a report it can also be used for input – to modify the records in the database.

When you create a screen two files are created: the screen file with the extension .SCR a format file containing the underlying dBASE III code – extension .FMT.

A format is therefore a special screen through which you can interact with a database. We are going to create a form or screen for the TRADCUST database. It will look like Figure 2.4.

It is possible to use such screens in conjunction with programs, as we will see in later Chapters.

 **Guided activities**

1. If you are starting a new dBASE session, make sure that TRADCUST is open for use – do not open an index file for this activity.
   Then move to the Create menu and select Format.
   Select the appropriate drive – a screen format should be on the same drive as the database (TRADCUST) to which it relates.
   When prompted, enter the name of the file as CUSTSCRN and press Return.
2. A special Format Design Screen appears – see Figure 2.5.
   There are 4 menu choices at the top of the screen – Set Up, Modify, Options, and Exit.

Use the Right and Left arrow keys to move across the menus – try this.

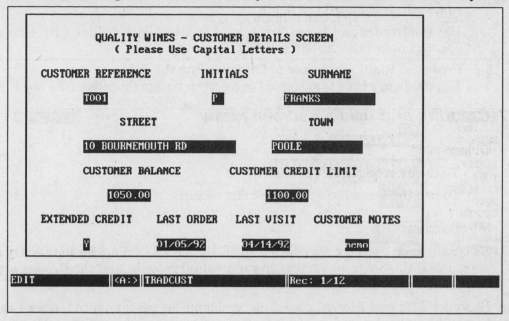

Figure 2.4

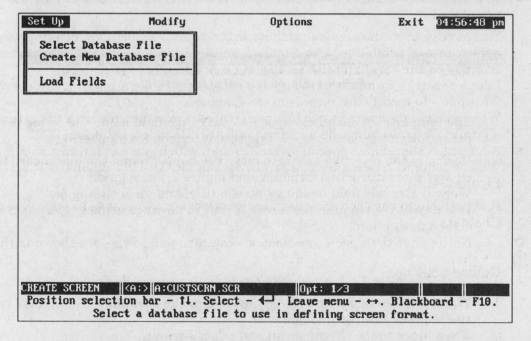

Figure 2.5

Each menu offers its own 'pull-down' choices when highlighted. The Up and Down arrow keys move up and down these choices.

Select an option in the usual way – by highlighting it and then pressing Return.

3.  Move to the Set Up menu and select the Load Fields option - a list of field names appears.

We are going to use this screen format to add or amend all the customer details, so we will include all the fields.

4. Use the Return and Down Arrow keys to select each field in turn – an arrow head appears next to each field selected.

5. Press the Right Arrow key to finish loading the fields.
   The fields are then transferred to a screen design 'blackboard' – see Figure 2.6.

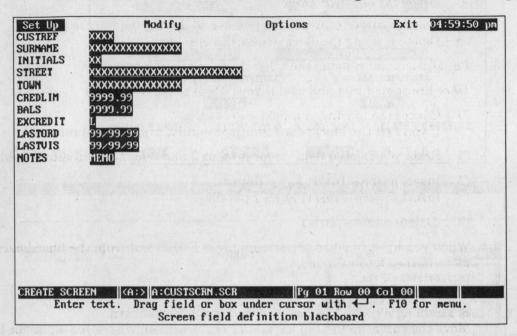

Figure 2.6

The template for each field appears next to the field name – showing the field's definition in the database – X's represent letters, 9's numbers etc.

6. Basically the objective now is to move the fields around the blackboard to create a clearer more attractive format, using Figure 2.4 as a guide.
   We will also add field headings, screen title, and an enclosing box.
   It is a good idea to plan the screen layout in advance using graph paper or a screen design form.
   Notice that the screen coordinates – columns and rows – are shown in the status bar.

   *Note. The Num Lock key should be off during screen design.*

   *The Insert key should also be off, except when inserting.*
   *Check these in the status bar.*

7. Follow these three basic steps for the NOTES field:

   a. *Move the field*

   Move the cursor onto the highlighted field template next to the field name.
   Press Return.
   Move the cursor to the screen position where the field is to start.

Press Return again – the field is re-positioned. Repeat if the field needs moving again.

b. *Add the field Heading*

Type the heading 'Customer Notes' above the NOTES field.

c. *Delete the old field name*

Use the cursor control keys to move to the old field name NOTES. Delete it using the Backspace or Delete keys.

8. Re-position and rename the other fields in the same way.

Here are some hints and useful keys if you make a mistake:

❒ Cancel the moving of a field – Press Esc.
If you exit the blackboard unintentionally, press F10 to return.

❒ Restore a deleted field – repeat steps 2 and 3 for the individual field.

❒ Insert a line – Insert key + Return
Insert spaces – Insert key + Spacebar.

❒ Delete a line – Ctrl-Y.

9. When you have finished the screen, press F10 to exit from the blackboard, and move to the Options menu.

10. *Drawing a box*

Select 'Single bar' – You are returned to the Blackboard.
Move the cursor to the top left corner of the screen, where you want the box to begin. Press Return.

11. Now use the Right arrow to move to the top right corner of the box.
*Do not press Return yet.*
Now move the cursor to the bottom right hand corner and press Return – the box should appear.

12. If the box is wrong, locate the cursor anywhere on it and press Ctrl-U – then repeat steps 9-11.

13. Finally, press F10 to return to the main menu, and select Exit and save.

**Independent exercises**

1. To retrieve and use the screen format, first make sure that TRADCUST is open.
Then move to the Set Up menu and select 'Format for Screen'.
Select the correct drive and file name next.

2. Now select Edit from the Update menu.
The first customer record is displayed using the screen format – see Figure 2.4.
Press Ctrl-Home to open the memo field and add a note.

3. Similarly the Append option will allow you to add a new record – try this.

---

**Summary of commands used**

At Assist

| | |
|---|---|
| *Format option from the Create menu* | Create a new Screen Format |
| *'Format for Screen' from the Set Up menu* | Retrieve a Screen Format |

In Screen Design Blackboard

| | |
|---|---|
| *Insert key + Return* | Insert line |
| *Ctrl-Y* | Delete line |
| *Ctrl-U* | Delete field |
| *Insert key + Spacebar* | Insert spaces |
| *F10 key* | Move between blackboard and menus |

---

## Activity 3 *Checking user input – data validation*

### Objectives

1. To modify a screen format.
2. To check data entered by the user.

### Introduction

When records are being added to the database, an important issue is data integrity – ensuring that the data is, as far as possible, complete and accurate.
In the case of the screen entry form that we have just designed, the user may make several types of data entry error:
He may enter letters in lower instead of upper case.
He may not use the correct format for reference numbers.
He may insert blanks instead of letters.
The value entered in numeric fields may be unreasonably high or low.
He may amend fields he is not authorised to amend.

We will trap these errors in the screen form, so ensuring that the information in the database is correct.

### Guided activities

1. If you are starting a new dBASE session, make sure that the date is set to UK format.
   Move to the Modify menu and select Format. Select the correct drive and file name – CUSTSCRN.SCR.
   The Format design screen appears – Move to the Set Up menu and select 'Select Database File'.
   Select TRADCUST – the database that the screen format is based upon.

2.  Now Press the F10 key and the screen blackboard appears.
    Notice that at the moment character fields such as CUSTREF, SURNAME and INITIALS are filled with X's.
    These allow any character – numbers, letters, and blanks to be entered – we will prevent this.

3.  Move the cursor onto the CUSTREF field and press F10.
    The Modify menu is now displayed.
    Select the 'Picture Functions' option – your screen will now look like Figure 2.7.

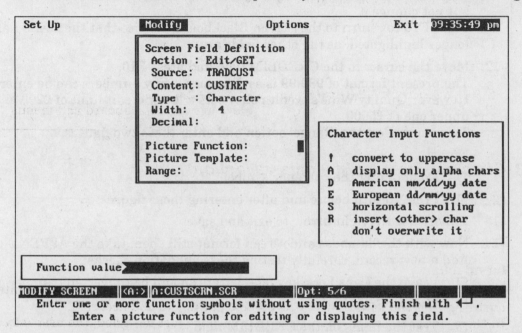

Figure 2.7

4.  Listed to the right of the screen are a list of character input functions.
    Bottom left is a data entry box; enter the '!' function and press Return.
    This will convert any letters entered into the customer reference field to upper case.

5.  Now Highlight the 'Picture Template' option.
    This displays a list of characters representing the picture or format the field should have.
    The CUSTREF field is one letter followed by 3 numbers, e.g. S001. Enter A999 in the data entry box and press Return.

6.  Press F10 to return to the blackboard, this time move the cursor to the INITIALS field and press F10.

7.  Repeat step 4 to convert characters entered to upper case.

8.  Repeat step 5 – this time enter the picture value as AA.
    This will ensure that the characters entered are alphabetic and contain no leading blanks.

9.  Continue this process for the SURNAME and TOWN fields in turn.
    They too must be all upper case and alphabetic. You will need to insert 15 A's in the Picture Template to correspond to their field lengths in the database.

10. The STREET field may be converted to upper case, but leave the Picture Template as X's (any character) as it will contain both the number and the street.

11. Move the cursor to the BALS field and press F10.
    We are going to prevent the user from editing this field, it will be updated by a special program – see Section 3, Chapter 8.
    Highlight the 'Action' option in the Modify menu. Press Return and the setting will change to 'Display/SAY'
    This makes the field a display only field – the user can see the customer balance but not change it.
    Press F10 to return to the Screen Blackboard – notice that the BALS field is no longer highlighted, as the other fields are.

12. Move the cursor to the CREDLIM field and press F10.
    The present format of 999.99 is satisfactory – only numbers can be entered.
    However Quality Wine's credit policy sets a lower credit limit of £200 and an upper one of £5000.
    This time select the 'Range' option and enter these two figures.

    Notes:

    ❐ Do not enter the currency symbol.

    ❐ Press Return before and after entering these figures.

13. Finally use the right arrow to exit and save.

14. Now with the database and screen format still open, take the APPEND option. Add a new record, carefully testing these validation checks:

    ❐ Leave the Caps Lock key off – letters should be converted to upper case.

    ❐ Use the Spacebar to try to enter spaces.

    ❐ Test the limits on the CREDLIM field.

### Independent activities

1. Modify the screen format CUSTSCRN as follows:

   Edit the EXCREDIT field so that the user can only enter an N or a Y.
   Edit the LASTORD and LASTVIS fields so that the user must enter dates in the UK format dd/mm/yy.

2. Test these changes using the APPEND option.

---

**Summary of commands used**

*Format option from the Modify menu*        Modify an existing Screen Format

Picture Functions and templates:

         !    *Convert lower to upper case*

         A    *Any alphabetic character*

---

| | |
|---|---|
| X | *Any character including spaces* |
| N | *Any alphanumeric character (letters or numbers)* |
| 9 | *Numbers or signs only* |
| Y | *Y or N only (logical fields)* |
| E | *Date fields in European (UK) format* |

# Activity 4 *Creating and using a view*

### Objectives

1. To view selected fields using a View file.
2. To view selected records using a View file.
3. To modify a View file.
4. To use screen formats and reports with Views.

### Introduction

You have already learned the general principles of data retrieval in dBASE – you have learned how to display, browse and delete records, and how to use field lists and build search conditions.

However Quality Wines may wish to run the same query at regular intervals, e.g. to display the names, addresses and credit details of customers who have exceeded their credit limits.

Entering the same search every time is time-consuming and unnecessary;

dBASE III allows you to create and store a special View File, specifying the fields to be displayed and the search conditions.

This can be used whenever needed, and also automates the tasks of opening databases and indexes before the query is run.

### Guided activities

1. If you are starting a new dBASE session, make sure that the date is set to UK format.
   Select View from the Create menu and select the appropriate drive.
   Call the view VIEW1.

2. The View Design Screen appears now with 5 main menu options along the top:

   Set Up     Relate     Set Fields     Options     Exit

   Select the TRADCUST database from the Set Up menu.
   Select the CUSNAME index from the list that appears.
   Both files should now be marked with an arrow head, indicating that they are selected for the view.

3. Press the Right Arrow key to move to the Set Fields menu.
   Press Return to select it, and a list of fields appears.
   At present all the fields are selected for inclusion in the view – marked with an arrow head.

4. Using the Down Arrow and Return keys, deselect all but the 4 fields we wish to include – SURNAME, INITIALS, CREDLIM, and BALS.

   The screen should now resemble Figure 2.8.

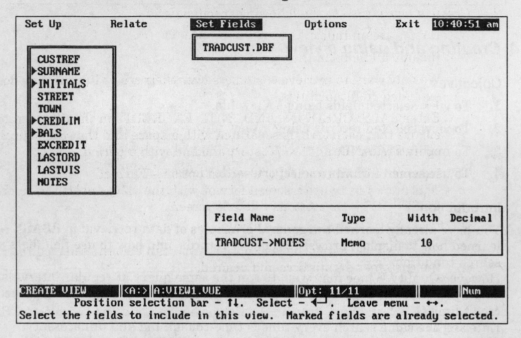

Figure 2.8

5. Press the Right Arrow key to move to the Options menu.
   Press Return to select the Filter option.
   This allows us to filter the records we want to include in the view – customers exceeding their credit limit.
   Enter BALS>CREDLIM and press Return again.

6. Finally press the Right Arrow key to move to the Exit menu. Select Save.
   Your view file VIEW1.VUE is saved to disk.

7. *Using a View*

   Move to the Set Up menu and select View.
   Select the correct drive and the view file VIEW1.VUE.
   Move to the Update menu and select Browse.
   A number of records will be displayed – note the effects of the view :
   Only the records meeting the filter condition are displayed – customers exceeding their credit limits.

   Only the fields selected are chosen. The records can be edited now, if desired.
   If no records are displayed then you have no records meeting these conditions – check the database.

**Independent activities**

1. *Modifying a View.*

    Move to the Modify menu and select View. Select VIEW1.
    Using the Set Fields option, add the CUSTREF field to the fields in the view.
    Exit, save and use the List option to display the records.

2. *Create a new view* – to the following specifications

    a. Do not use an index.

    b. Include all fields in the view.

    c. We only want to retrieve customers over their credit limit if they don't get extended credit facilities.

       Enter BALS>CREDLIM .AND. .NOT. EXCREDIT in the filter option – ensure that each term is separated with a space and that the logical operators .AND. and .NOT. start and end with a period.

    d. Now move down to select the second option – Format
       This allows us to use a screen format with the view. Insert the screen format CUSTSCRE – the customer details screen.

    e. Exit and save this view as VIEW2.

    f. Run this view using the Edit option – you can edit the selected records using the customer details screen if desired.

3. *Using a View with a report.*

    Now VIEW2 is set up, move to the Retrieve menu and run the report CREDREP (see Activity 2).
    The Report will now be displayed or printed with the filter conditions specified in VIEW2 – i.e. only customers who do not have extended credit facilities will be included in the report of customers exceeding their credit limit.

---

**Summary of commands used**

At Assist

| | |
|---|---|
| *View option from the Create menu* | Create a new View |
| *View option from the Modify menu* | Modify an existing View |
| *View from the Set Up menu* | Retrieve a View |

*Edit, Browse, List and Display options can all be used in conjunction with a view.*

---

## Section 2

# dBASE IV – using the Control Center

Section 2 is entirely concerned with the menu-driven mode of dBASE IV – the Control Center.

dBASE III users should omit this section and continue with Section 3, Chapter 6.

# Chapter 3

# Creating and searching a database

---

**Introduction to chapter**

*In the next three Chapters you will learn how to perform data management tasks using the Control Center – the menu system that appears when you first enter dBASE IV.*

*This is the easiest method for new users, as you can choose all the commands that you need from a series of menus.*

*From Chapter 6 onwards the dot prompt is introduced, which allows you to enter commands directly on the screen.*

---

 ## Getting started

To run dBASE IV you need:

- ❐ a hard disk drive with at least 3.5Mb free disk space (dBASE IV version 1.5. needs 4 Mb.)
- ❐ 640k of main memory (RAM) free
- ❐ DOS version 2.1 or later.

If you are working independently and are unsure about any of these then you will need to seek guidance.
If you already know how to start up dBASE IV then skip to Activity 1.

Turn on the computer, but do not insert a disk yet.
When you see the prompt C> or C:\> or similar, type the word DBASE and press the Return or Enter key.
This large key is to the right of the keyboard and is usually marked with a curled arrow.
If this does not work then it is probable that the dBASE IV package has been installed in its own directory.
Do the following: Type DIR/W after the C> prompt, and press the Return key.
The directory for the hard disk is displayed. Look for a directory with a likely name, e.g. DBASE, or DBASE4.
Change to this directory by typing the letters CD followed by a space and the directory name, e.g. CD DBASE
Press the Return key. Now type DBASE and press Return again.
This will run dBASE IV.

## Activity 1 *Displaying and using the Control Center*

### Objectives

1.   To use the dBASE IV Control Center.
2.   To use the Help system.
3.   To exit from the Control Center to dot prompt.

### Introduction

The Control Center, as its name suggests, is your key to the rest of the menu system. From the menu system you can gain access to data, issue commands, design screens and reports, and many other tasks.

In your first activity you will learn the basic functions of the Control Center and how to find your way around it.

### Guided activity

### Entering dBASE IV

1.   On entering dBASE IV (see above – Getting Started) the first thing you will see is the license agreement screen.
     Press the Return key. The Control Center screen appears – see figure 3.1.

```
 Catalog    Tools    Exit                                    5:35:50 pm
                      dBASE IV CONTROL CENTER

                   CATALOG: C:\DBASE4\UNTITLED.CAT

    Data        Queries        Forms        Reports       Labels      Applications
 ┌───────────┬───────────┬───────────┬───────────┬───────────┬───────────┐
 │ <create>  │ <create>  │ <create>  │ <create>  │ <create>  │ <create>  │
 │           │           │           │           │           │           │
 │           │           │           │           │           │           │
 │           │           │           │           │           │           │
 │           │           │           │           │           │           │
 │           │           │           │           │           │           │
 │           │           │           │           │           │           │
 └───────────┴───────────┴───────────┴───────────┴───────────┴───────────┘
 File:        New file
 Description: Press ENTER on <create> to create a new file


   Help:F1  Use:◄─┘  Data:F2  Design:Shift-F2  Quick Report:Shift-F9  Menus:F10
```

Figure 3.1

2.   If the Control Center has not appeared, it may be that your computer has been set up differently – see 'Getting Started' above.
3.   If the screen is displaying the dot prompt – a full stop followed by a blinking cursor – press the F2 function key on the keyboard.
     You may find that you accidentally end up at the dot prompt in later activities – the F2 key will always take you back to the Control Center.

## Navigating the Control Center

1.  In the centre of the screen are 6 panels containing the 6 main options:

    Data, Queries, Forms, Reports, Labels, Applications.

    These are the six types of applications that you can create in dBASE IV.

    dBASE IV *(version 1.5) – using a mouse*

> Mouse users –
>
> If you are using version 1.5 and have a mouse installed on your computer then you will see the screen pointer, displayed as a block on the screen.
> You have the option of using the mouse to select a menu option or to issue a command.
> Users of earlier versions of dBASE IV can perform exactly the same tasks by using the arrow keys to highlight a menu choice, then pressing the Return key.
>
> For the first few activities in this Chapter I'm going to give the instructions for non-mouse users first, followed by mouse-user's instructions in a box (like this section). Use whichever you prefer.
> Later on, when you've mastered menu selection, I shall be using the word 'select' for both mouse and non-mouse selections.
> There are three basic mouse operations, if your mouse has more than one button, use the left button to carry these out:
>
> a.  'Click' – move screen pointer to selection, press button once and release.
>
> b.  'Double Click' – move screen pointer to selection, press button twice in quick succession and release.
>
> c.  'Drag' – hold down button and move mouse to highlight or move object.
>
> When you first start using the mouse it may feel clumsy and imprecise, you will soon improve with practice.

Don't worry if the layout and choices seem rather daunting at first, we will deal with each element as it arises.
If this is your first session then each panel will only contain the word Create. Later on the names of files that you have created will appear below.

2.  At the moment the first option – Data – is highlighted.

    Press the right and left arrows and observe how the highlight changes as each option is selected.

> Mouse users – click once to move the screen pointer to the <Create> option in each column.
> If you double click and select an option by mistake, don't worry. Press the Esc key, and click the 'Y' on the prompt box that appears. You will be returned to the Control Center.

**Independent activities**

1. *The Help Option*

   Explore the Help option as follows:
   In the Control Center move to the first menu option – Data, and highlight the Create option as above.
   Press the Function key F1 – the Help key.

   > Mouse users – click the word Help at bottom left of the screen.

   A Help box appears giving information on the Create option.
   dBASE IV offers context-sensitive help. i.e. it gives you information appropriate to where your cursor or highlight is currently located, or the stage you have reached.
   Use the F4 key to move to the next help screen and explore the rules for field names and file creation.

   > Mouse users – click the word 'Next screen' at the bottom of the screen.

   Make sure that you can use the other help keys and menu options listed in the summary of commands at the end of this activity.
   Press Esc to exit Help.

2. *Exiting from dBASE IV*

   To exit from dBASE IV, first press the F10 key. This will take you to the menu bar at the top of the screen.
   Use the right arrow to move to the Exit option. The first option 'Exit to Dot Prompt' will already be selected.
   Press Return to select it, and you enter dot prompt mode.

   > Mouse users – move the pointer to the Exit menu and click. Then click the option 'exit to dot prompt'.

   You may do something while working in the Control Center that inadvertently causes you go to the dot prompt.
   If so, simply press the F2 function key at the top of the keyboard – do this now.

   You are returned to the Control Center. Now use the F10 key to take the Exit option again. This time highlight the option 'Quit to DOS' and press the Return key.

   > Mouse users – click the Exit menu again. This time click the option 'Quit to DOS'

   This will exit from dBASE IV back to the operating system.

*Always exit from the Control Center in this way, it closes down any files you may be using. Merely turning off the computer and/or ejecting your disk will damage your files irretrievably.*

---

**Summary of commands used**

| | |
|---|---|
| *F1* | Call Help |
| *F2* | Return to Control Center from dot prompt |
| *F4* | More information on the current topic |
| *F3* | Previous screen on current topic |
| *F10* | Open menus at the top of the screen |
| *Esc key* | Exit Help or the Control Center |
| *Contents Option* | Displays list of Help topics |
| *Backup Option* | Displays previous Help topic |
| *Print* | Prints current Help text |

---

# Activity 2 *Defining the database structure*

### Objective

To create a database and define its structure.

### Introduction

As the first computerisation step, Quality Wines is going to create a simple database of its trade customers.

It has the structure shown in Figure 3.2.

| Field 1 Surname | Field 2 Initials | Field 3 Street | Field 4 Town | Field 5 Credit Limit | Field 6 Balance | Field 7 Last Order | Field 8 Last Visit |
|---|---|---|---|---|---|---|---|
| FRANKS | P | 10, BOURNEMOUTH RD | POOLE | 1000 | 1050 | 01/05/92 | 14/04/92 |
| SMITH | JB | WEST DOCKS | SOUTH'N | 750 | 100 | 22/04/91 | 28/05/92 |
| HARRIS | A | 8, WEYMOUTH RD | POOLE | 200 | 3000 | 17/04/92 | 18/05/92 |
| SMITH | P | 7, GOLDEN SQUARE | BOURNEMOUTH | 300 | 000 | 10/12/91 | 12/04/91 |
| ALI | G | 6, CHRISTCHURCH RD | BOURNEMOUTH | 500 | 200 | 07/06/92 | 16/06/92 |
| PATEL | M | 10, KING ST | SOUTHAMPTON | 450 | 300 | 08/02/92 | 20/11/91 |

Figure 3.2

To recap briefly on the database terminology used in the Introduction:

There are 6 customer *records* in the *database* or *file*. All contain the same *fields* or items of information. Some fields contain only alphabetic *characters*, others only *numeric* information, and others dates.

The field *values* differ between records
e.g. FRANKS, SMITH.

### Guided activities

Planning the database fields – their names, length and type, is the first step of database design. This has already done for you in Figure 1.2.

We can now use dBASE IV to define the database structure.

1.  Enter the Control Center as you did in Activity 1.
    First make sure that the highlight is on the Create option in the Data column.
    Press the Return key to execute this choice.

> Mouse users – move the pointer to the Create option in the Data column and click.

If you make an error and choose the wrong option the Esc key will take you back a step.
You will be taken into the screen shown in figure 3.3.
It allows you to define the various fields in the database.
The line immediately below the column headings is highlighted, ready for you to define your first field
The cursor always shows you where you are up to.

```
 Layout   Organize   Append   Go To   Exit                  5:44:51 pm

                                              Bytes remaining:    4000

  Num   Field Name   Field Type   Width   Dec   Index

   1    ▮▮▮▮▮▮▮▮▮    Character    ▮▮▮    ▮▮▮    N










 Database║C:\dbase4\<NEW>            Field 1/1
            Enter the field name. Insert/Delete field:Ctrl-N/Ctrl-U
 Field names begin with a letter and may contain letters, digits and underscores
```

Figure 3.3

2.  The first field name is SURNAME – key this in.
    Notice that it appears in upper case.
    Press the Return key to move to the next column – Field Type

> Mouse users – move the pointer to the next column and click – do this from now on instead of pressing Return.

SURNAME is a character field, i.e. it consists of letters. Character is the default setting (what you get unless you change it), so merely press Return to confirm it and move to The next column – Width.

The maximum length of a surname will be 15 characters. Type 15 and press Return again.

The next column option – Dec (for decimal places) only applies to numeric fields, so you are moved to the final column – Index which is preset to N.

We are not going to index any of the fields at this stage, so accept this default and press Return.

> Mouse users – move the pointer to the Field Name column.
> Click immediately under the first field name – SURNAME.

3.  You have now defined your first field, and are moved to the next line, ready to define the second field.
    The second field is the customer's initials – INITIALS.
    This is a 2 character field, not indexed.
    Define this field in the same way as you did the first.

4.  *Correcting Mistakes*
    ❐ The left and right arrow keys – move a character at a time
    ❐ Return or Tab key – move forward a field at a time
    ❐ Shift and Tab keys together – move back a field

> Mouse users – simply click on the field or character that you want to change.

    ❐ Delete key or Space bar – delete characters – (or type over unwanted characters)
    ❐ Insert key – insert missing characters – press it again to turn it off when you have finished.

5.  Now define the third field – STREET as 25 characters, and the fourth field – TOWN – as 15 characters.

6.  The cursor should be now located at the fifth field name, this is the customer's credit limit – CREDLIM.
    Key this name in and press Return. This is our first numeric field; press the space bar and the default setting, Character, will change to Numeric.
    Press Return to confirm this.

> Mouse users – click on the field type 'Character' once to select it, click again and it will change to 'Numeric'.

53

No customer's credit will be more than £5000. This requires a field width of 4 digits. (currency symbols cannot be stored in numeric fields).
Key in 4 and press Return, and, enter 2 in the Dec column As before, accept the Index setting as N.

7.   The sixth field we will call BALS – the customer's outstanding balance, i.e. the amount they currently owe to Quality Wines.
Alter the field type to numeric as before.

As the company has fixed the largest permissible debt at £5000.00, we will allocate it a total field length of 7 (6 digits and the decimal point)

This time complete the Dec column by entering 2 for the 2 decimal places, and again accept the index setting as N.

8.   The seventh field is the date of the customer's last order.
As an experiment try to enter LAST ORDER DATE as a field name.
You will find that the spaces are not allowed.
Field names must consist of 10 letters, numbers, or less and contain no spaces.
The underscore character can also be used, but not the dash.
Alter the field name to LASTORD.
dBASE IV uses a special field type to store dates.
When your cursor is located on the second column, Field Type, press the space bar until you see 'Date' appear.
Press Return to confirm.

> Mouse users – click on the field type 'Character' once to select it, click until it changes to 'Date'.

It is allocated a standard length of 8. (the format dd/mm/yy = 8 characters)

*When you move on to a new field, you may accidentally press the Return key twice in succession and receive the prompt on screen 'Save as'. If this happens don't worry, merely press the Esc key, and carry on defining fields.*

Two other field types – logical and memo fields - will be dealt with in later chapters.
Now complete the eighth field LASTVIS, which stores the date that the customer was last visited by a company representative.
Follow the same procedures as for the previous field – LASTORD.

9.   You have now defined 8 fields, the status bar at the    bottom of the screen shows:
     [ Database ] [ C:dbase4\<NEW> ] [ Field 9/9 ]

Press the up and the down arrow keys, and the first digit of 9/9 changes as you move between fields.
< NEW > means that the database has no name yet.

Press the Return key with the cursor located on line 9, and you are prompted for a file name.
File names in dBASE IV can be up to 20 characters long, but it is best to restrict them to 8, as this is the maximum length that DOS, the computer's operating system, can recognise.
File names, like field names, can consist of numbers, letters or underscores but not dashes or blanks.

We are going to assume that you will be saving your work to drive C – the hard disk.

If you want to save it to drive A, then you must preface the file name with A: (capital A followed by a colon)

If you are doing this then you must have a suitable formatted disk in the external drive A.

Type A: now if you are going to use A drive.

As it is our trade customer database call it TRADCUST.

Press the Return key, and you will be prompted, 'Input Data Records Now? (Y/N)'.

Enter N and you are returned to the Control Center.

```
 Catalog    Tools    Exit                                   5:57:26 pm
                         dBASE IV CONTROL CENTER

                     CATALOG: C:\DBASE4\UNTITLED.CAT

      Data        Queries      Forms       Reports     Labels     Applications
 ┌────────────┐┌────────────┐┌────────────┐┌────────────┐┌────────────┐┌────────────┐
 │ <create>   ││ <create>   ││ <create>   ││ <create>   ││ <create>   ││ <create>   │
 │ TRADCUST   ││            ││            ││            ││            ││            │
 │            ││            ││            ││            ││            ││            │
 │            ││            ││            ││            ││            ││            │
 │            ││            ││            ││            ││            ││            │
 │            ││            ││            ││            ││            ││            │
 │            ││            ││            ││            ││            ││            │
 └────────────┘└────────────┘└────────────┘└────────────┘└────────────┘└────────────┘

 File:        A:\TRADCUST.DBF
 Description:


 Help:F1  Use:◄┘  Data:F2  Design:Shift-F2  Quick Report:Shift-F9  Menus:F10
```

Figure 3.4

Notice that the name of the database that we have just defined is displayed in two places – see Figure 3.4.

In the Data column – as the first and only member of a list of databases.

At the bottom of the screen – plus the file type extension .DBF (database file).

This indicates that TRADCUST is the 'active' database – the one currently in use.

Move the up arrow and the database is 'deselected' and the Create option is selected – ready for you to create another database.

10. Highlight TRADCUST to reselect it, and then press the function key F10.

> Mouse users – click the menu 'Catalog' at the top of the screen.

You are taken into the menu bar at the top of the screen, and the first of the three options – Catalog.

Press the up/down arrow keys to highlight the sub-option 'Change Description of Highlighted File'.

Press Return.

> Mouse users – move the screen pointer onto the top or bottom border of the
> Catalog menu; the pointer becomes an arrow.
> Click to highlight each choice in turn.
> Click the sub-option 'Change Description of highlighted File'.

Type the description 'Trade Customer Master Database'. Press Return again.
It is a good idea to enter a brief description to remind you of the purpose of a
database; in a business environment you may have many files listed in the
Control Center, often with similar 8 character file names.
The description now appears next to the file name in the Control Center.

11. Let us now amend the date format for the LASTORD field if necessary.

    DBASE IV is an American-produced package and the US standard date format is
    mm/dd/yy – difficult if you are used to the UK format dd/mm/yy.

    Press the F10 key again, but this time use the right arrow key to select the Tools
    option.
    Highlight the Settings sub-option, and press Return.

> Mouse users – move the screen pointer onto the 'Tools' option at the top of
> the screen and click. Then highlight the 'Settings' sub-option.

Now find the Date Order option in the list that appears. If it is already selected as
DMY then no action is required.
Press the Esc key to return to the Control Center.
If any other option is displayed do the following:
Move down to highlight this option. Press the space bar/click with mouse until the
DMY option scrolls into view.
Now use the right arrow key to move to the Exit option and press Return to
return to the Control Center.
End your dBASE session at this point, – select the Exit option using F10 or the
mouse as you did in the previous session.

## Activity 3 *Entering data into the database*

### Objectives
1. To change the drive.
2. To enter six records into the TRADCUST database.
3. To amend database records.
4. To close a database when not needed.

### Introduction
At the moment we have an empty database – a structure with no contents.

We will be adding records for some of Quality Wines trade customers.

**Guided activities**

1. If you are starting a new dBASE IV session, you should start at the Control Center.

   Look at the Catalog Line towards the top of the screen. It reads 'CATALOG' followed by either the letter A: or C:

   A is the floppy disk/diskette drive, C the internal hard disk. Either might be the default drive.

   As mentioned in Activity 2, we shall assume that you are saving your work on the hard disk — drive C.

   However, if you are saving to a floppy disk — drive A, you will need to know how to change your default drive.

   Make sure that you have a suitable diskette in the floppy disk drive — drive A. Now follow these instructions:

2. First press the F10 key — this takes you to the pull-down menus at the top of the screen.

   Using the right arrow key, highlight the Tools option. Then highlight the sub-option 'DOS utilities', and press the Return key to select it.

   The Dos Utilities screen appears listing the files on the present drive. Press F10 again.

> Mouse users — click the Tools option at the top of the screen.
> Click the sub option 'DOS utilities'.
> Now click the DOS option at the top of the screen.

   This takes you to the DOS menu.
   Select the option 'Set default drive:directory'.
   Now use the Delete key to erase the present default and enter the drive letter A: or C:

   If you want to save your work to its own directory, then follow the colon with a \ symbol and directory name and press Return, e.g. A:\dbase4.
   From now on all your work during will be saved to this drive.

   Use the Esc key to return to the Control Center. (answer Y to the confirm prompt). Ensure that you are on the correct drive each time you re-enter dBASE IV for a new session — see the status bar at the bottom of the screen.

   *From now on I shall be assuming that you have mastered the two basic steps of making a menu choice — i.e. Use the arrow key to highlight the choice, Press the Return key to select.*

> *Mouse users — locate the screen pointer on choice, click to select it.*

   *I will be using the word 'select' to refer to these two steps.*

3. The database that we created last session — TRADCUST — is displayed in the Data column of the Control Center.

Make sure that it is highlighted and press the Return key to select it.

| *Mouse users – double click on TRADCUST* |
| --- |

A further menu 'window' appears now, select the first option, 'Use file'.
(Note: if TRADCUST is already open, then you will see the option 'Close file' – in this case press Esc to exit this window)
You will notice that the name TRADCUST is above the line in the data column of the Control Center, confirming that the database is in use – see Figure 3.4.

4.   Study the options listed along the bottom of the screen, now press F2 to select the 'Data' option.
The Edit screen is displayed. This is a template, showing the fields that you have defined in the previous activity - see Figure 3.5.
The fields and field widths for the TRADCUST database are shown as blank areas next to the field names.
Enter the 6 customer records shown in Figure 3.2 *using capital letters.* (use the Caps Lock key).
Enter the data exactly as shown, it will be important in our later activities.

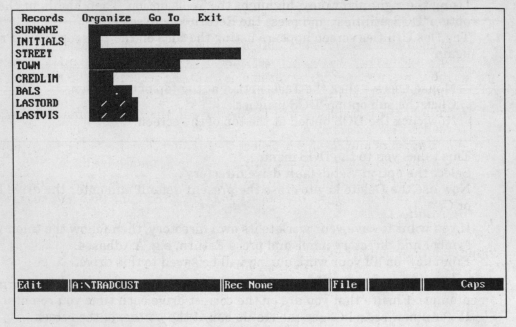

Figure 3.5

5.   Notes:

❐   If you make a mistake use the arrow keys or mouse and overtype.
The Delete, Backspace and Insert keys can also be used.

❐   If the data that you enter completely fills the field then the cursor will automatically advance to the next field.
Otherwise you must press the Return key or use the mouse.

❐   Be careful to distinguish the digit 1 from the capital letter I, and the digit 0 from the capital letter O.

❑ Enter the date in the UK format discussed above, dBASE will prevent you from entering an invalid date.

When you have completed the last field of the first record, the template will become blank again, ready for the next record.

If you need to return to a previous record use the up arrow or the PgUp key. The down arrow and PgDn keys move you forward in the database.

6. After you have entered 2 records, press the F2 key and you will be taken into the Browse screen; this shows the fields horizontally across the screen as a table. Enter two more records in this mode, press F2 again and return to Edit screen. From now on use whichever screen that you prefer. The Browse screen is best for the rapid review and editing of large number of records, the Edit screen for individual records.

When you have finished entering the records, the status bar will confirm the number of records in the database – 6.

7. To exit and save these records do *one* of the following:

❑ Press the Ctrl and the End keys together, or

❑ Select the Exit option from the menu bar at the top of the screen.

You will exit to the Control Center.

8. *Closing the database*

It is good policy to close any database when it is not being used.

When a database is open for use, some of its contents are in main memory. If the power should fail, then some or all of the records can be damaged – closing it makes sure that its contents are written to disk.

Highlight the Database name TRADCUST in the Data column if necessary, and press Return/click mouse.

A box appears on the screen. Select the option 'Close file '. The name now appears below the horizontal line, indicating that the database is closed.

*Make sure that you close databases you are not using in future activities – you do not need to do this if you are exiting from dBASE IV, as they will be closed automatically.*

**Independent activity**

In this activity you will learn a central database maintenance tasks – editing or amending records.

Starting at the Control Center, select the TRADCUST database, (see Guided Activity above).

When the menu window appears, select the third option – 'Display data'.

The Browse screen appears, showing the 6 records already added, see Figure 3.6. If the Edit screen appears press F2.

If only the last record is displayed press the Pg Up key. Now carry out the following amendments, using the editing keys shown in the summary.

a. Amend the last visit for HARRIS to 20/06/92

b. Alter FRANKS's credit limit to 1100.

c. Alter the last order date for ALI to 08/07/92

Exit and save as before, and exit dBASE.

```
┌─────────────────────────────────────────────────────────────────────┐
│ Records   Organize   Fields   Go To   Exit                            │
│ ┌──────────┬─────────┬──────────────────┬─────────────┬───────┬─────┐ │
│ │ SURNAME  │ INITIALS│ STREET           │ TOWN        │CREDLIM│ BAL │ │
│ ├──────────┼─────────┼──────────────────┼─────────────┼───────┼─────┤ │
│ │ FRANKS   │ P       │ 10 BOURNEMOUTH RD│ POOLE       │  1000 │ 105 │ │
│ │ SMITH    │ JB      │ WEST DOCKS       │ SOUTH'N     │   750 │  10 │ │
│ │ HARRIS   │ A       │ 8 WEYMOUTH RD    │ POOLE       │  2000 │ 300 │ │
│ │ SMITH    │ P       │ 7, GOLDEN SQUARE │ BOURNEMOUTH │   300 │     │ │
│ │ ALI      │ G       │ 6, CHRISTCHURCH RD│ BOURNEMOUTH│   500 │  20 │ │
│ │ PATEL    │ M       │ 10 KING ST       │ SOUTHAMPTON │   450 │  30 │ │
│ │          │         │                  │             │       │     │ │
│ └──────────┴─────────┴──────────────────┴─────────────┴───────┴─────┘ │
│ Browse   A:\TRADCUST          Rec 1/6      File            Caps       │
└─────────────────────────────────────────────────────────────────────┘
```

Figure 3.6

---

**Summary of commands used**

In Edit or Browse screens:

| | |
|---|---|
| *F2* | Change between EDIT and BROWSE screens |
| *Return, arrow & mouse keys* | Move between fields |
| *PgUp and PgDn keys* | Move between records |
| *Delete and backspace keys* | Delete data |
| *Insert key* | Insert data |
| *Ctrl and End keys together* | Exit and save database |

---

# Activity 4 *Information retrieval 1 – viewing selected fields*

## Objectives

1. To create a View using the Queries Design Screen.
2. To list selected fields.

## Introduction

Quality Wines now have a small database of trade customers.
Occasionally it may be useful to list or print the whole database, i.e. all customers, all fields, but a commoner business need is to retrieve only certain records. For example:

Only customers living in Poole – for reps. visits.

Only those who have exceeded their credit limit – for the Credit Controller.

Or a particular customer, e.g. to change his/her address

Typically one does not need to view the whole record, but only certain fields, e.g. the customer's name, address, and date of last visit.
dBASE IV handles queries by allowing you to build Views.
A view is a special type of query which shows you selected records and fields from one or more databases.

## Guided activities

1.  First you need to ensure that the TRADCUST database is open for use:
    Select TRADCUST from the Data column of the Control Center, then select the option 'Use file'.
    Now move to the Queries column and select the Create option.
    The Query Design Screen appears as in figure 3.7

```
 Layout    Fields    Condition    Update    Exit              6:52:37 pm

 Tradcust.dbf ↓SURNAME  ↓INITIALS  ↓STREET  ↓TOWN  ↓CREDLIM  ↓BALS  ↓LASTORD  ↓L
 ████████████

  ┌View─
  │<NEW>          Tradcust->     Tradcust->     Tradcust->     Tradcust->
  │               SURNAME        INITIALS       STREET         TOWN
  │                                                                         ──→

 Query    C:\dbase4\<NEW>        File 1/1                            Caps
  Next field:Tab  Add/Remove all fields:F5  Zoom:F9  Prev/Next skeleton:F3/F4
```

Figure 3.7

2.  The screen is divided into two main parts.

    At the top of the screen is the 'file skeleton' i.e. the names of the fields in the TRADCUST database.
    At the bottom of the screen these fields are repeated as the 'view skeleton', i.e. the names of the fields that can be included in the final 'view' or query.
    Initially all the fields are shown in the view skeleton, but the design screen allows you to select out the fields that you want to display or to print.
    At the moment there are too many fields to fit on screen at once.

61

3. Moving around the design screen is mainly controlled by the function keys, (top row), and the Tab key – usually at the top left of the keyboard and marked with opposite - facing arrows.

> Mouse users – change between fields and skeletons simply by clicking .
> See summary of commands for these.

First press the F5 key a couple of times. This makes the view skeleton at the bottom of the screen disappear and reappear.
This will not work unless the highlight is located on the file name at the top left of the screen – in this case TRADCUST.
Next press the F4 key – this moves you between the two skeletons at the top and bottom of the screen.

4. Now use the Tab key – this will move you from field to field.
Do this on the view skeleton at the bottom of the screen. You will see the fields scroll into view from the right of the screen.
Hold down the Shift key and press Tab to reverse the direction.

5. The simplest case is where we want to view all eight fields.
When you first enter the View screen this is exactly what we get – all fields are automatically selected.

Press the F2 key and, after a few seconds to process the view request, the database is listed in Browse mode on the screen.
Press F2 again and you are taken into single record Edit mode.
Pressing F2 yet again returns you back to Browse mode. You can edit or add records in either mode.
Press the Shift and F2 keys together and you return to the Query Design Screen.

6. For our second view of the database, remove the present view skeleton using the F4 and F5 keys as mentioned above, i.e. use F4 to move to the file skeleton, at the top of the screen.
Press Tab to locate the highlight on the file name.
Press F5 twice to remove the present view. The bottom of the screen should now be blank.

7. We are going to add the fields we want one by one to create a new view.
Use the Tab key to move to the first field in the file skeleton – SURNAME.
Press the F5 key.
The field is placed at the bottom of the screen – the first field to be added to the file skeleton.
Repeat this for the next three fields, INITIALS, STREET and TOWN.

We have now finished our second view.
Use F2 to display this view, and Shift-F2 as before to return to the Query Design Screen.

8. To start another new view proceed as before:
Use F4, if necessary, to move to the file skeleton, and then locate the highlight on the file name.

Press F5 to remove the present view.
Produce another view, this time of SURNAME, INITIALS and BALS.
View it as before, then return to the design screen.

9. Another way to produce views is by deleting fields from the view skeleton.
Delete the old view as before, and, with the file name still highlighted, press F5 to insert all the fields at the bottom of the screen.
Now remove the last two fields from the view skeleton; proceed as follows:
Highlight the field name LASTVIS on the file skeleton.
Press F5 and the field disappears.
(If you delete the wrong field then repeating the two above steps will reinstate the field, at the end of the view skeleton)
Repeat for the LASTORD field.
Using F2, display this view, and use Shift F2 to return to the View screen.

Note: deleting fields from the view does not delete them from the database; on the other hand, any amendments that you make to the fields when the view is displayed, may be saved.

## Independent activities

1. Create the following views using F2 to check that the correct fields are displayed in the correct order. (use Shift-F2 to return to the design screen)

   a.  Customer names, addresses, and date of last order.

   b.  Customer surnames, towns, and current balance.

   If the fields appear in the wrong order, a field may be moved as follows:

   Highlight the field in the view skeleton.
   Press F7 to select the field.
   Use the Tab key to move the field to its desired location
   Press Return to place the field there, Esc cancels the move.

2. End your session as follows:

   Select the Exit option at the top of the screen. Although it is possible to save a view we will not do so in this case.
   Select' Abandon changes and exit' – enter 'Y' to confirm.
   You are returned to the Control Center.

---

### Summary of commands used

*In designing Views use the following function keys:*

| | |
|---|---|
| *F2* | Display a view |
| *Shift-F2* | Return to the View Design screen |
| *F4* | Move between the View and File skeletons |
| *Tab* | Move forward along skeleton |
| *Shift-Tab* | Move backwards along skeleton |

---

| | |
|---|---|
| *F5* | Insert or delete a field from the view |
| *F5* | On the database file name at the start of the file skeleton, delete an old view skeleton and insert a new one. |
| *F7* | Selects a field that you wish to move |
| *F10* | Activates the menu at the top of the screen |
| Mouse users – | |
| *Click field* | Highlight field in file skeleton |
| *Click top border of field* | Highlight field in view skeleton |
| *Double click the field name in the file skeleton* | Add field to/remove field from view skeleton |

## Activity 5 *Information retrieval 2 – viewing selected records*

### Objective

To retrieve and display only records that meet certain search conditions.

### Introduction

In the previous activity we selected the fields we wanted to include in a view.
The next stage is to select only those records that meet certain search conditions. e.g only customers living in Poole, or only those who have exceeded their credit limit.
Eventually we will combine both activities and view only certain fields of certain records. This is a very common business requirement.
dBASE IV uses a feature called Query By Example – QBE.
The user queries the database by entering an example of the field value for which he is searching.

### Guided activity

If you are starting a new dBASE IV session then open the database TRADCUST for use, and select the Create option from the Queries column as before (see Activity 4).
The Queries Design Screen appears.
Let's first briefly recapitulate the layout of the screen – see Figure 3.7.
Along the top of the screen is the file skeleton showing the fields of the database TRADCUST.
Along the bottom of the screen is the view skeleton that contains the same fields – all or any of which can be included in the view you are creating.
To activate the menus at the top of the screen press F10.
Use the arrow keys plus return to select a menu option.

> Mouse users – click the menu and the options to select them.

1. *Searching on numeric fields.*
   First, as a simple example, let's view all customers with a balance of 200.
   Go to the file skeleton at the top of the screen, move to the BALS field and type 200.
   Select F2, and one record is displayed – G ALI is the only customer where the BALS field = 200.
   Note that it is not necessary to type the = sign.
   Now return to the View screen (Shift-F2) and the value 200 is still displayed.
   Alter the search condition to <1000, and select F2 as before.
   4 records should be displayed – those customers where the balance is less than 1000.
   As before you can use F2 to change from Browse to single record mode.

2. Using the View screen, amend the search condition to >3000, and the message 'no records selected' appears – there are no customers with a balance of more than 3000.

3. *Searching on character fields*
   To search a character field, such as the surname or town, requires that the text be enclosed in quotes (single or double).
   Erase the previous search conditions as follows:
   Highlight the BALS field and then press the Ctrl and Y keys together – do this whenever you change the field that you are searching on.
   Now enter the value 'SMITH' in the SURNAME field of the file skeleton, using the quotes and in upper case.
   Activate the query as before, and two records are displayed.

4. *Searching on more than one field*
   It is possible to search on more than one field at once, simply by entering values under two or more of the fields.
   Erase the previous search condition, and enter > 400 under the CREDLIM field.
   Now enter 'SOUTHAMPTON' under the TOWN field.
   Next press the F2 key and the one record will be selected that meets both these search conditions.
   Erase these search conditions and repeat these steps to find the customer that lives in Bournemouth who has a zero balance.

5. *Searching on date fields*
   Searching the LASTORD field, a date field, requires that the date be enclosed in curly brackets.
   Erase any search conditions.
   View customers that haven't ordered since 1991 by entering <{01/01/92} in the LASTLORD field
   Pressing F2 displays the customer records where the LASTORD field has a value of less than 01/01/92.
   Similarly locate customers that have ordered on or after 05/03/92.
   'Greater than or equal to' is represented by the sign '>='

6. *Substring searching*

You may have noticed that Southampton has deliberately been entered in two ways – SOUTHAMPTON and SOUTH'N

This is bad practice as a normal search using 'SOUTHAMPTON' as the search term would not retrieve 'SOUTH'N' (and vice versa)

However we can overcome this by searching on part of the name – a substring. Erase previous search conditions (Ctrl and Y keys)

Enter $'SO' in the TOWN column of the file skeleton.

Press F2 and the view displays the 2 Southampton customers, SMITH and PATEL.

7. *'AND' and 'OR' conditions*

So far we have combined search conditions using the implied logical connector 'AND', i.e. both search conditions must be present for a record to be selected.

It is also possible to search using the condition 'OR', e.g to locate customers that live in either Southampton or Bournemouth (clearly 'AND' is inappropriate here, a customer must live in one or the other)

We have already inserted the search condition for TOWN = $'SO'.

Keeping the highlight on this field, press the down arrow, and the column dividers are also extended.

Now enter the second search condition – 'BOURNEMOUTH', press Return, and use F2 to display the view.

All Southampton or Bournemouth customers will be displayed.

Repeat these steps to locate customers named Smith or Patel.

8. *Creating new fields by calculation*

A further useful feature is to create new fields in your report by means of calculation.

For instance it is very useful to know which customers have exceeded their credit limit, and by how much.

There is no point in storing this permanently in a database when it can be calculated as and when needed.

First erase the previous search, and start a new view skeleton, and include the following fields; SURNAME, INITIALS, CREDLIM, BALS. (see previous activity if you need guidance)

To add a calculated field proceed as follows:

Move to the Fields menu. Select the 'Create calculated field' option.

Enter BALS-CREDLIM in the window provided. (– is the minus sign)

Press Return to finish defining the calculated field.

Now press F5 and you are prompted for the name of this new field, call it OVERLIMIT.

Press Return again.

The field is now created and is moved to the view skeleton at the bottom of the screen.

Use the F2 key to display this new view.

Return to the Query Design Screen.

9. Now open the Layout menu
   Select the option 'Edit description of query'
   Enter the description, 'balances compared to credit limits'.

10. Now run this query and save it under the name VIEW1 as follows,
    Move to the Exit menu and take the option 'Save changes and Exit'.
    Enter the name VIEW1 at the 'Save as' prompt.
    When you return to the Control Center VIEW1 is listed in the Queries column,
    and the description appears beneath.

## Independent activities

Make sure that the TRADCUST database is opened for use, and then create a new
view – select the Create option on the Queries panel of the Control Center as before.

Let's now combine the skills that you have gained from this and the previous activity:

1. Firstly select only the following fields to be displayed in the view;
   SURNAME, INITIALS, STREET, TOWN, BALS.
   Refer back to Activity 4 if you need to refresh your memory.

2. Now select only customers where the balance is either 100 or less or 2500 or more
   – i.e. customers with large or small balances.
   Enter a description for this view.
   Save this query as VIEW2.
   Exit to the Control Center.

3. *Running a saved Query*

   Select the query file VIEW2.
   When the prompt box appears, select 'Display Data'. Exit from this view using the
   Esc key.

4. *Modifying a saved Query*

   Select the query file VIEW1.

   When the prompt box appears, select 'Modify Query'.
   The View screen will appear next, amend the query so that it applies only to
   Poole customers.
   Amend the description of the view too.
   Now run this query and check its correctness.
   Return to the design screen.
   Open the Layout menu.
   Select the option' Save this query' and save it under the new name VIEW3.
   Now exit to the Control Center.
   When you return to the Control Center both the original query, VIEW1, and the
   modified query, VIEW3, will be shown.

**Summary of commands**

Symbols and Operators Used in View Screen

| | |
|---|---|
| = | *not needed, merely enter the value under the field name* |
| < | *less than* |
| > | *greater than* |
| <> | *not equal to* |
| >= | *greater than or equal to* |
| <= | *less than or equal to* |
| $ | *contains (followed by a text string in quotes)* |
| + | *addition* |
| – | *subtraction* |
| * | *multiplication* |
| / | *division* |
| Ctrl-Y | *erase a search condition.* |

# Chapter 4

# Modifying and reorganizing the database

**Introduction to the chapter**

*In this Chapter you will learn three important skills:*

*a.  adding additional fields to hold new information,*

*b.  maintaining the database by adding, deleting and editing records, and,*

*c.  placing the records in a new order by indexing and sorting.*

## Activity 1 *Modifying the database structure*

### Objectives

To add new fields to the TRADCUST database.

### Introduction

At present the TRADCUST database consists of six records.
Each record is divided into 8 fields SURNAME, INITIALS, etc
We are going to modify this structure by adding new fields.

### Guided activity

1.  If you are starting from the Control Center, select the appropriate drive and the TRADCUST database – see previous Chapter if you need guidance.
    Select the option 'Modify structure/order' from the menu window that appears.
    The present fields are displayed – see figure 4.1.
    If necessary press the Esc key to clear any pull-down menu that may overlay this screen.

2.  We are going to insert a field to hold the customer's reference number.
    Highlight the SURNAME field and press the Ctrl and N keys together.
    A blank field appears above the surname field.
    Name this field CUSTREF and define it as a character field, length 4 characters. Leave the index default as N.

3.  We will now create a second new field which will indicate if a customer gets extended credit facilities or not.
    All we wish to store is a single character, Y for yes, or N for no.
    Highlight the LASTORD field, and press Ctrl-N again. Type in the field name EXCREDIT. Move to the Field Type column.
    Now press the Space Bar to change the field type to Logical, and press Return to confirm.

```
 Layout    Organize    Append    Go To    Exit                    5:05:18 pm

                                                          Bytes remaining:   3916
 ┌─────┬──────────────┬──────────────┬───────┬───────┬─────────┐
 │ Num │ Field Name   │ Field Type   │ Width │ Dec   │ Index   │
 ├─────┼──────────────┼──────────────┼───────┼───────┼─────────┤
 │  1  │ SURNAME      │ Character    │  15   │       │    N    │
 │  2  │ INITIALS     │ Character    │   2   │       │    N    │
 │  3  │ STREET       │ Character    │  25   │       │    N    │
 │  4  │ TOWN         │ Character    │  15   │       │    N    │
 │  5  │ CREDLIM      │ Numeric      │   4   │   0   │    N    │
 │  6  │ BALS         │ Numeric      │   7   │   2   │    N    │
 │  7  │ LASTORD      │ Date         │   8   │       │    N    │
 │  8  │ LASTVIS      │ Date         │   8   │       │    N    │
 │     │              │              │       │       │         │
 └─────┴──────────────┴──────────────┴───────┴───────┴─────────┘
 Database  A:\TRADCUST                     Field 1/8
               Enter the field name. Insert/Delete field:Ctrl-N/Ctrl-U
 Field names begin with a letter and may contain letters, digits and underscores
```

Figure 4.1

> Mouse users – click to change the field type to Logical; then click next
> column.

A logical field is always one character long and can hold the values T for true or F
for false, or, if preferred, Y for yes or N for no.

Decimal points and indexing do not apply to logical fields

4. Next use the down arrow key or mouse to move past the last field.

   In the blank space provided, create a new field NOTES (it will be used to hold
   notes about each customer).

   Define this field as a memo field, it is automatically allocated a width of 10
   characters, but allows you to store up to 512k of notes about each customer record
   in a related record.

   Decimal points and indexing do not apply to memo fields.

5. The only field type that we have not used in the database is Float.

   Short for floating point, it offers greater precision than Numeric fields for certain
   scientific purposes.

   We shall not be using it for the business examples in this book.

6. Press the down arrow again and room for a 12th field is added.

   To delete this unwanted field, make sure that it is highlighted and press the Ctrl
   and U keys together.

7. Move to the Exit menu at the top of the screen, using F10 or the mouse.

   If you are satisfied that the changed structure is correct then take the option
   'Save changes and exit'. (press Return to confirm)

   If you have made any serious errors and deleted fields, it is better to take the
   other option 'Abandon changes and exit '. Then repeat the above steps.

   This will keep the database as it was before.

   Remember that if you delete a field any information held in it will be deleted too.

---

**Summary of commands used**

Modify Database Structure Screen:

| | |
|---|---|
| *Ctrl-N* | Insert a field |
| *Ctrl-U* | Delete a field |
| *Tab / Shift-Tab* | Move forward/back a field |

---

# Activity 2 *Adding and deleting records*

### Objectives

1.  To add new records to the TRADCUST database.

2.  To delete records from the TRADCUST database.

3.  To restore deleted records.

### Introduction

At the moment the TRADCUST database contains only six records. We shall be increasing this number to about 20, and also entering information in the new fields that we have created in the previous exercise.

### Guided activity

1.  Select the TRADCUST database; when the menu window appears take the third option 'Display data'.
    Make sure that you are in Browse mode – press F2 if not.
    If necessary use the up arrow key or mouse to move to the first record.
    The six records should now be displayed, as in figure 4.2.
    Notice that the 3 new fields, CUSTREF, EXCREDIT, and NOTES are currently blank – use the Tab key or mouse to scroll all 3 fields into view.

2.  Complete the CUSTREF and EXCREDIT fields as follows:

    (Use the Caps Lock key so all the new information is entered in upper case.)

    ❏   CUSTREF – enter the reference number T001 for FRANKS, T002 for SMITH JB, etc.

    ❏   EXCREDIT – enter Y in this field for FRANKS and HARRIS, N for the other 4 customers.
    Remember that you can toggle between single record edit or full screen Browse mode using the F2 key.

3.  *Completing Memo fields*
    Memo fields allow us to attach blocks of information to a record that would be inconvenient in a fixed length field.

| Records | Organize | Fields | Go To | Exit | | |
|---------|----------|--------|-------|------|--|--|

| CUSTREF | SURNAME | INITIALS | STREET | TOWN | CRE |
|---------|---------|----------|--------|------|-----|
| ▓▓▓▓ | FRANKS | P | 10 BOURNEMOUTH RD | POOLE | 110 |
| | SMITH | JB | WEST DOCKS | SOUTH'N | 75 |
| | HARRIS | A | 8 WEYMOUTH RD | POOLE | 200 |
| | SMITH | P | 7, GOLDEN SQUARE | BOURNEMOUTH | 30 |
| | ALI | G | 6, CHRISTCHURCH RD | BOURNEMOUTH | 50 |
| | PATEL | M | 10 KING ST | SOUTHAMPTON | 45 |

| Browse | A:\TRADCUST | | Rec 1/6 | File | | | Caps |
|--------|-------------|--|---------|------|--|--|------|

Figure 4 .2

We are going to use the NOTES field to store notes on a few of the customers.
At the moment the word 'memo' appears in lower case, indicating that the field is empty.

4. Highlight the NOTES field of the first record and press the Ctrl and Home keys together.

   A word processing screen appears. Type the notes:

   1. Do not send monthly statement.
   2. Always obtain owner's personal signature for deliveries.

   Press the Ctrl and End Keys together, the text is saved, and you are returned to the Edit or Browse screen.
   'MEMO' now appears in upper case, showing that it contains information.
   Use the same operations if you want to amend a memo field.

5. *Copying Memo Fields*
   Copy the information from the NOTES field of the first record to the NOTES field of the second record as follows:
   Highlight the NOTES field of the second record and press Shift and F8 keys together.
   Check that the copy operation has worked by opening the memo field as above.

6. *Adding records*
   Now add at least 10 more records to the TRADCUST database.
   To add a new record press the down arrow until you get the prompt 'Add new records? (Y/N)'
   Supply the details yourself, but make sure that:

   a. There are two J WILSONs both in the town WEYMOUTH.

   b. There is one customer in the town DORCHESTER.
      These will be used in later searches of the database.

Note: As you will recall, the menus at the top of the screen can be opened by using the F10 key. Menu options are then selected by highlighting them, and pressing Return.

> Mouse users – Menus at the top of the screen, and their options can be selected by locating the screen pointer on them and clicking.
> The options at the bottom of the screen can also be selected in this way, e.g. F2 and Shift-F2.

7. *Deleting individual records*

   From time to time customer records may need to be deleted
   You can do this in either Browse or Edit screens.
   Highlight record 10 – check its number on the status bar.
   Open the Records menu.
   Select 'Mark record for deletion' and 'Del' appears on the right of the status bar at the bottom of the screen.
   Notice that the record has not disappeared – this is because dBASE IV only *marks* the record for deletion initially, it does not actually remove it at this stage. It can then be either recalled, or erased permanently.

8. To unmark the record, first make sure that record 10 is still highlighted, then select 'Clear deletion mark' from the Records menu.
   The 'Del' flag has disappeared from the status bar.

9. *Erasing deleted records*

   Highlight record 5, and this time use the quick delete method – press the Ctrl and U keys together.
   'Del' should appear in the status bar as before.
   Press Ctrl-U again and the record is unmarked.
   Finally press Ctrl-U a third time to mark it again.
   Now move to the Organise menu.
   Select the 'Erase Marked Records' option.

   *Warning. This operation will remove the record permanently - the record cannot be restored.* A panel appears asking you to confirm this. In this case we will not go ahead, so answer N.
   Press Esc to clear the pull-down menu.

10. *Deleting groups of records*

    Often we want to delete groups of records sharing common characteristics, e.g. all records for customers that have not placed an order since a certain date.
    Rather than browse a large database picking them out manually we can build a query – see Chapter 3, Activities 4 and 5.

11. Exit to the Control Center and make sure that the TRADCUST database is still selected for use.
    Then move to the Queries panel and select the Create option
    The Query Design Screen will appear now, showing the fields in the TRADCUST database – see Chapter 3, Activities 4 and 5.

12. Use the Tab key to move to the LASTORD field, and enter the search condition
    <(06/06/91)
    Press F2 to review the records that your query has selected, and check that they match your search condition.
    Press Shift-F2 to return to the Query Design screen.

13. Now select the Update menu at the top of the screen.

    Select 'Specify update operation' and then select the sub- option 'Mark records for deletion'.
    A prompt box appears explaining that the view skeleton will disappear if you proceed.
    Select the Proceed option. The word 'mark', under the file name confirms that the records will be marked for deletion.
    Now move to the Update menu again, and select the option 'Perform the update'
    A message box asks you to confirm this – answer Y (plus Return)

14. Press any key to continue, and you are returned to the Query Design screen.
    Now that the group of records is marked for deletion, you have the choice, as with individual records, of unmarking them or removing them permanently from the database.

15. *Unmarking groups of records*

    Press the F2 key to go to the Browse or Edit screen.
    Move to the Organise menu and select the option 'Unmark all records'

16. *Erasing groups of records marked for deletion*
    We will not erase any records at this stage.
    Doing so would involve selecting the 'Erase marked records' option from the Organise menu.

17. Press Shift-F2 to go to the Queries Design Screen
    Open the Layout menu and select the option, 'Edit description of query'.
    Enter a suitable description and press Return.

18. Open the Exit menu, and select
    'Save changes and exit'.
    Save the query as DEL1.

## Independent activity

Build a query to delete all the Dorchester customers.
Erase the record(s) permanently, and browse the database to check that it has been removed.
Save the query as DEL2.

| Summary of commands used | |
| --- | --- |
| *Ctrl-Home* | Open memo field |
| *Ctrl-End* | Close and save a memo field |
| *Shift-F8* | Copy contents of memo field from previous record |
| *Ctrl-U* | Mark/unmark a record for deletion |

# Activity 3 *Indexing the database*

## Objectives

1.   To create indexes for the TRADCUST database.
2.   To display records in indexed sequence.

## Introduction

A common business need is to present the same information in a variety of orders,
e.g. a list of customers either in name or town order.

At the moment our database is in serial or unordered sequence – i.e. the records are in
no particular order. This makes it difficult to search once it gets over a certain length.
First we are going to index the database on the Town field, so for example, all the
Bournemouth customers will be grouped together, followed by all the Dorchester
customers etc.

The field that is used to organise a file into a particular sequence is called the *key field*
or *record key*.

As we will see later it is possible to index a file on more than one key, e.g. in surname
order within town. Town would then be the primary key, and surname the secondary
key.

Then by way of contrast we will look briefly in Activity 6 at the second major method
of reorganising database records – sorting.

Sorting works by physically rearranging the records and storing them in a second
database, leaving the original database unchanged.

Indexing works by creating an index file containing the pointers to database records.
This has the advantage of economising on disk space – only a small index file is
needed to access the database in a new sequence.

Sorting records into a new database gives faster access to them than using an index
(this is not noticeable in the small databases we are creating) at the price of
duplicating the information over two databases.

But if one database is changed then the other then the other needs updating too if it is
not to become inconsistent.

With indexing however the various indexes are automatically updated whenever
records are changed or added.

 ## Guided activity

1.   Starting from the Control Center, make sure that the TRADCUST database is
     highlighted.
     Press the Shift and F2 keys together and the screen shown in Figure 4.3 appears.

2.   The Organise menu should already be open, so merely press Return to select the
     option 'Create new index'
     A submenu appears next – see figure 4.4.

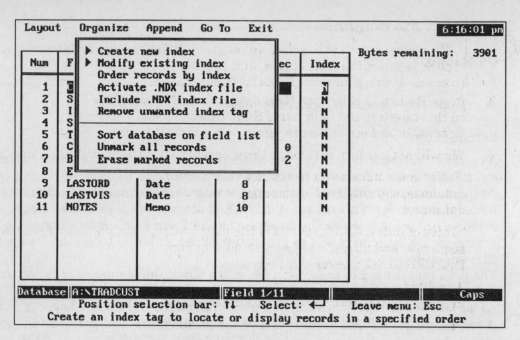

Figure 4.3

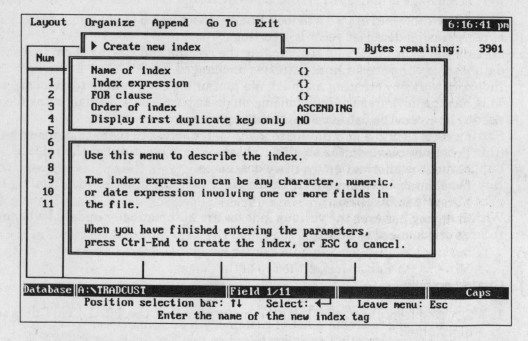

Figure 4.4

First of all press Return or click mouse to select the first option, 'Name of index'. As we are going to place the customer records in surname order, call the index CUSNAME.

Index names can be up to 10 characters long, but it is best to keep them short, simple and descriptive.

Press Return again.

> Mouse users – click to select an indexing option, enter the information, then
> click to select the next option, and so on.

3.  Press Return to select the Next option – 'Index expression'
    In this case it is the field name SURNAME
    Enter this and press Return again.

4.  We will not use any of the last three options yet, briefly explained they are:

    'FOR clause' allows you to restrict your indexing to a subset of records in the
    database, e.g. only Poole customers – this would be especially useful in larger
    databases.

    'Order of index' ASCENDING is the usual order, i.e. alphabetic fields in a – z
    sequence, and numeric in low to high sequence.
    DESCENDING reverses this sequence.

    'Display first duplicate key only' allows you to hide records with duplicate key
    field values, e.g. records with duplicate customer reference fields.

5.  Press Ctrl and End keys together to save this index.
    A message is displayed, 'Index on SURNAME TAG CUSNAME 100% indexed'.
    Each index created is identified by its name or 'tag'.
    It is stored in a main index file which has the same name as the database that it
    indexes.
    So in this case the index file containing the CUSNAME index is
    TRADCUST.MDX.
    .MDX is the file extension for all main index files.

6.  You are now returned to the database design screen.
    Press the F2 key and the records will be displayed in surname order – either in
    Edit or Browse mode.
    Make sure that you are in Browse mode and press the up/down arrows to move
    from record to record.
    Notice that the current record numbers appearing in the status bar are no longer
    in numeric sequence.
    This is because the records remain in the same physical sequence in the database,
    but are now displayed in a new order using the index that we have just created.
    Move to the Exit menu at the top of the screen.
    Select 'Return to database design'.

7.  *Indexing on more than one field*
    We are going to create a list of customers in surname order within town.
    This involves creating an index based on two key fields. i.e. TOWN is the primary
    key field, within which the records are ordered by SURNAME, the secondary key.
    Repeat steps 2- 6 above, but this time call the index NAMETOWN, and enter
    TOWN+SURNAME as the index expression.

8.  *Combining fields of different data types*
    It is possible to create an index using character, numeric or date fields (but not
    memo or logical fields).

Sometimes we want to combine different field types as an index expression, e.g. order the customer records by the date of their last visit, within town.
TOWN the primary key is alphabetic, but LASTVIS the secondary key is a date field.
We must convert the date to characters using a special dBASE function DTOS (date to string).
A number of these functions are included in the summary of commands at the end of this exercise.

9. Create this new index following steps 2 – 6 above, calling the index VISTOWN.
Under the Index expression option enter TOWN+DTOS(LASTVIS)
Now display the records in this new order.

## Independent activities

1. Create a new index on the CUSTREF field, call it CUSTREF.
Use it to display the records in customer reference order.

2. Create a new index on the BALS field, in order to display customer records in order of their balance. Call this index BALANCE.
Display the records in this new order and return to the Control Center.

---

### Summary of functions used

*STR(<FIELDNAME>,<LENGTH>) e.g. STR(CREDLIM,4)*

         converts numeric fields to character fields

*DTOS(FIELDNAME)*    converts date fields to character fields

*UPPER(FIELDNAME)* converts lower to uppercase letters for indexing purposes

---

# Activity 4 *Modifying, activating and deleting indexes*

### Objectives
1. To modify an existing index.
2. To call up and use an existing index.
3. To delete an unwanted index.

### Introduction
Now that we have created several indexes to the TRADCUST database we need to know how to use and maintain them.
The following activities cover modifying, using and deleting indexes.

**Guided activity**

1.  *To modify an existing index*

    At the Control Center, make sure that TRADCUST is highlighted in the Data column, and press Shift-F2.

    The Organise menu appears already open – see Figure 4.3.
    Select the option 'Modify existing index' and a list of indexes appears.
    Select the BALANCE index, and press Return.

2.  The present settings for the BALANCE index are displayed.
    Highlight the 'Order of index' option and press the space bar (or click with mouse) to change the setting to Descending.
    This allows you to display customers with the largest debts first.
    Press the Ctrl and End keys to save.

3.  Now press F2 to display the records in this modified order. The records are now displayed from highest to lowest balance.

4.  *To activate an existing index*

    At the moment the customer records are displayed using the BALANCE index – the last index opened.
    It is useful to be able to redisplay it in a new order.
    Move to the Organise menu and select the option, 'Order records by index'.
    A list of indexes appears, select the NAMETOWN index – the records are automatically redisplayed in this new order.

5.  *Deleting an index*

    As dBASE IV automatically updates indexes whenever a key field is altered, removing unwanted indexes improves processing times.

    Move to the Organise menu, and select the option, 'Remove unwanted index tag'
    Select the VISTOWN index.
    Finally press Esc to close the Organise menu.
    Exit to the Control Center.

# Activity 5 *Searching for individual records*

### Objective

To locate individual records in the database.

### Introduction

So far we have searched the database, either by browsing for individual records, or creating views of records sharing common characteristics.
We shall be learning a third way, in order to locate individual records quickly.

**Guided activity**

1. Open the TRADCUST database and display the records in Browse mode, using F2.
   Move to the 'Go to' menu on the menu bar, and select the first option 'Top record '.
   This moves the database file pointer to the first record.

2. Repeat this operation for the second 'Go to' option – and move to the last database record.

3. Let's now search for a record by a field value.
   Move the highlight to the SURNAME column, and select the 'Go to' menu again.
   As the last record is presently selected, select the 'Backward search' option.
   Enter the field value SMITH in the 'Enter search string' box.
   The backward search finds the first surname Smith.
   Press Shift-F3 to locate the next – remember that the original 6 customer records contained 2 Smith's.

4. Press Shift-F4 to search forward and locate the other Smith again.

5. Another useful feature is the ability to search on either lower or upper case.
   With the SURNAME field still highlighted, move to the first record.
   Select the forward search option, this time entering the search string 'wilson' in lower case.
   You will get a 'Not found' message as the surname WILSON is stored in upper case.

6. Returning to the 'go to' menu, you will notice that the final option is 'Match capitalization'.
   Press the Space Bar/click the mouse to alter the default to No.

7. Now Highlight the 'Forward search' option again, and press Return – this time the record for Wilson is located.
   Press Shift-F4 to locate any other Wilson's.

   Note. You can only use this search facility with character strings.

8. *Using an index and the * wild card*

   With large databases it is quicker to use an index when searching.
   Open the Organise menu, and select the option 'Order records by index'.
   Select the CUSNAME index.

9. Now, using the 'Go to' menu as before, move to the top record of the database.
   Let's say that we are uncertain, say, whether a customer's name is FRANK or FRANKS.
   Make sure that the Surname column is still highlighted.
   Open the 'Go to' menu again and select 'Forward search'.
   Enter the Search string FRAN*
   The correct record is located – the asterisk or 'wild card' character can stand for any combination of characters following the string FRAN.

### Independent activity

With the NAMETOWN index still open, search the TOWN field for Southampton customers.
Abbreviate the text string to Sou* – you will also need to check the 'Match capitalization' option is set to 'No'.

---

**Summary of commands used**

In conjunction with the 'Go to' Menu:

*Shift-F3 / F4*    Continue forward or backward search.

---

## Activity 6 *Sorting the database*

### Objective

To sort the TRADCUST database into a new order.

### Introduction

On occasions it may be useful to produce a copy of a database, sorted into a new order – although this means having to maintain two separate databases.
We are going to create a copy of TRADCUST, sorted by customer reference within town.
As customer references, names and addresses do not change frequently, this could be useful, when printed out, for cross-referencing customer names and reference numbers.

### Guided activity

1.    Starting from the Control Center, make sure that the TRADCUST database is highlighted, then select Shift-F2

2.    The database records are displayed now, either in Edit or Browse modes.
      Open the Organise menu and select the option, 'Sort database on field list'.

3.    Now press Shift-F1 for a list of possible sort fields.
      (the fields NOTES and EXCREDIT are memo and logical fields respectively, and cannot be used to sort).

4.    We are going to create a new database sorted on customer reference within town. Select TOWN, the primary sort field. The field name will now appear in a window, as in figure 4.5.

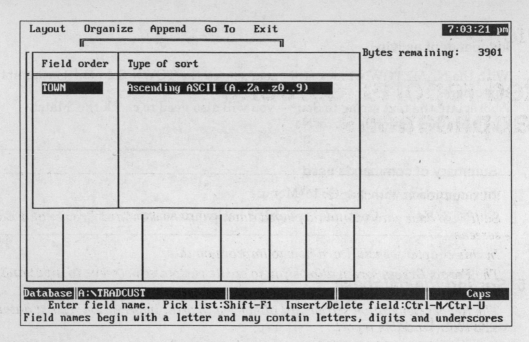

Figure 4.5

5.    Highlight the second column 'Type of sort'.
Press the space bar/click mouse a few times and you will see that there are 4 types of sort sequence:

Ascending and Descending ASCII – these two treat upper and lower case characters differently – capital letters come before lower case.
In general it is best to use one of the latter two sorts – Ascending or Descending Dictionary, which ignore differences in case, e.g. 'POOLE', 'Poole' or 'poole' are all treated similarly.
Select Ascending Dictionary and press Return.

6.    Now repeat the above operations for our secondary sort field CUSTREF.
Finally press Ctrl-End to save this file.
You will be prompted for a file name, call the new database CUSTREF.

7.    The sort now takes place and you will be prompted for a description of the new CUSTREF database.
Enter 'TRADCUST sorted by customer reference within town'

8.    Use the Exit menu to return to the Control Center, where the new database CUSTREF is listed in the data column.
Highlight it and press F2 to display the records.
Check that the records are sorted correctly.

### Independent activity

The CUSTREF database only needs the fields CUSTREF, SURNAME, STREET, TOWN. Delete the other fields.
Do this by selecting the database, and choosing 'Modify structure/order' from the window that appears.
Then delete the unwanted fields – see Activity 1.

# Chapter 5

# Printed reports, screens and applications

---

**Introduction to the chapter**

*So far we have entered and displayed data using the standard Browse and Edit screens.*

*In this chapter we will learn how to improve on this.*

*The Forms Design screen allows you to create customised screens to input and output data.*

*The Report Generation screen will allow you to print information from a database as a clear readable report.*

*You will also use the Application Generator to produce a main menu so that users can select the database task they require – browse, append, edit, delete etc.*

---

## Activity 1 *Creating a quick report*

### Objective

To print a quick report from the TRADCUST database.

### Introduction

To produce a report you must first select a database or view for the report to use. If you want the records displayed in a particular sequence, then the correct index must be open for use too.
In DBASE IV you can produce either a quick report or a professionally formatted 'custom' report.
A quick report merely prints all the records in the database or view, with the field names acting as column headings, any numeric fields are summed at the end.
No further formatting is possible, e.g. title, or subheadings.
If the report is based on a database rather than a view then all the fields will be printed.
A quick report is useful for brief checking of data.

 **Guided activity**

1.  Starting at the Control Center, highlight the TRADCUST database in the Data panel.
    Press Shift-F9.

2. The Print menu appears next, which we will examine further in the next activity. Do *one* of the following:
   a. If you are connected to a printer, select the first option, 'Begin printing'
   b. If there is no printer available, then select the third option, 'View report on screen'.

3. It will take some time for the report to be generated, line by line; this is a drawback to quick reports.

   When the quick report is produced, you will see the other drawback – poor display and readability.

   As there are too many fields to fit on one line, they 'wrap round' to the next line, making the report difficult to read.

4. Press Esc to return to the Control Center.

### Independent activity

Use the view VIEW2 to produce a quick report. You will find it more readable, as only the fields in the view appear in the report.

---

**Summary of commands used**

*Shift-F9*          Create quick report, based on the selected database or view.

---

## Activity 2 *Creating a custom report*

### Objective

To produce a formatted report based on the TRADCUST database.

### Introduction

In this activity we will produce a credit report on Quality Wine's trade customers. We shall improve on the quick report layout and include features such as date, title, column headings, subtotals and totals.
Part of the finished report is shown in Figure 5.1.

### Guided activity

1. First we need to open the index BALANCE to place the records in descending order of balance.
   Starting at the Control Center, highlight the TRADCUST database, and press Shift-F2.

2. Select 'Order records by index' from the Organise menu.
   Now select the BALANCE index from the list displayed.
   Finally exit to the Control Center.

3. At the Control Center, move to the Reports column, and select 'Create'.
   The Reports design screen appears, as shown in Figure 5.2.
   Press Esc to close any pull-down menu that may overlay it.

```
              Customer Credit Report on :-20/02/92

       Balance      Surname        Initials     Customer Reference

      4356.44 CR    MUIR           J            T015
      3000.00 CR    HARRIS         A            T003
      2034.34 CR    CARPENTER      L            T010
      1234.56 CR    WILSON         J            T013
      1050.00 CR    FRANKS         P            T001
       700.00 CR    WILSON         J            T007
       401.00 CR    MAITLAND       I            T012
       400.00 CR    CRAVEN         J            T011
       345.00 CR    MARSDEN        AG           T014
       345.00 CR    HOOD           S            T008
       300.00 CR    PATEL          M            T006
       234.00 CR    TANSEY         S            T016
       200.00 CR    ALI            G            T005
       100.00 CR    SMITH          JB           T002
         0.00       SMITH          P            T004
     14700.34 CR


            Cancel viewing: ESC,   Continue viewing: SPACEBAR
```

Figure 5.1

```
 Layout   Fields   Bands   Words   Go To   Print   Exit            3:30:42 pm
[·······▼·1····▼····2··▼·····3·▼·········▼·5·····▼····6···▼······7·▼·······
Page      Header   Band——————————————————————————————————————————————————

Report    Intro    Band——————————————————————————————————————————————————

Detail             Band——————————————————————————————————————————————————

Report    Summary  Band——————————————————————————————————————————————————

Page      Footer   Band——————————————————————————————————————————————————




Report   ║A:\<NEW>              ║Band 1/5       ║File:Tradcust║          Ins
            Add field:F5   Select:F6   Move:F7   Copy:F8   Size:Shift-F7
```

Figure 5.2

4. The Report Design screen appears rather daunting initially.
   Identify the following first:

   a. 7 menu options at the top – Layout, Fields etc (activated by pressing F10 or clicking with mouse).

   b. Below the menu bar is the ruler, the [ symbol represents the left-hand page margin.

    c.    The small triangles are the tab stops to set columns.
The Tab key advances one tab stop at a time.
Shift-Tab moves back one tab stop at a time.

    d.    The numbers 1,2,3 etc. on the ruler mark the column positions 10,20,30 etc.

5.    There are 80 column positions on a screen and the standard A4 printer.
First we will create a margin 5 columns wide on either side of the page.

Use F10 to open the Words menu at the top of the screen, and select the Modify Ruler option.
The cursor is now placed on the ruler line.
Move to column 5 and press the [ key to relocate the left margin.
Move the cursor to column 75, and repeat this operation, using the ] key to relocate the right margin.

6.    Now use the down arrow key ↓ or mouse to move to the next line.
The main area of the screen consists of 5 bands, used to define different sections of the report. Below each band heading is a shaded area for you to define each part of the report.
We will explain each band when we get to it.
For the moment press F1 for a brief explanation of each. (Esc to exit Help.)

7.    *Report Headings*

Press the down arrow again and you are located on the shaded area below the Page Header Band – notice that the status bar shows the new position of the cursor – Line: 0 Col: 0.

8.    The Page Header is the band used for the report title and column headings.
Move the cursor to column position 5, and type the title 'Customer Credit Report on:'.

9.    We will now insert the system date (maintained by the computer's internal clock).
Press the F5 key and the Add a Field window appears – see Figure 5.3.
It is divided into 4 columns, the first column showing the fields in the TRADCUST database.

10.    Move to the third column, containing predefined fields, and select Date.
A further window appears allowing you to alter the appearance of the field in the report.
Accept the default settings by pressing the Ctrl-End keys. You will now see the date placed on the Page Header Band as DD/MM/YY.

11.    Now we will centre the report title.
Open the Words menu, and select the Position option.
Another window opens – select the Center option.
The heading is now centred, press the End key to move to the end of the heading.

12.    The rest of the Page Header Band holds the column titles.
This allows us to use titles like 'Customer Balance', rather than the field name BALS.
Press the Return key twice to insert 2 blank lines in the header.

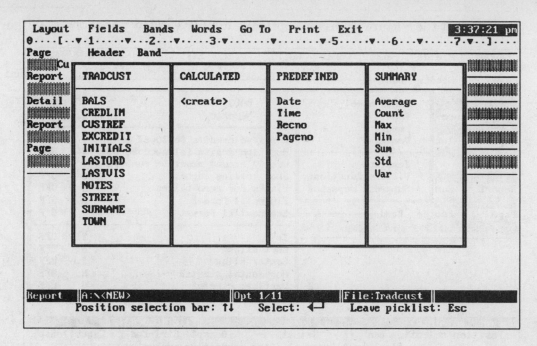

Figure 5.3

Move to column 5 on the line.
Now type these 4 column headings in the report and space them as follows:

    Balance     Surname              Initials    Customer Reference

They are spaced to allow for the different field lengths, e.g. SURNAME is a longer
field than INITIALS and BALS.
Notes:

❐ Use the right arrow, Tab keys or mouse to place them at suitable points on
the line.

❐ Use the Ins key and Space Bar if necessary to insert characters.

❐ Delete or Backspace key to remove characters.
Take care to keep within the left and right page margins that you have
defined.

❐ To add or remove a line use the 'Add line' or 'Remove line' options in the
Words menu.

13. When you have entered this line, press End then Return to create another blank
line in the Header Band.
We have now finished defining the headings – which will appear at the top of
every page in the report.

14. *Report Columns*

Press the down arrow to move to the shaded area below the Detail Band heading.
This is where we define the fields that appear in the main body of the report –
customers' initials, surname etc.
With the cursor located in column 5, press the F5 key.
The Add a Field window appears – see Figure 5.3 above.
Highlight and select the BALS field – a further window appears allowing you to
alter the appearance of the fields in the report.

Select the Picture Functions option; a further window appears – see Figure 5.4.

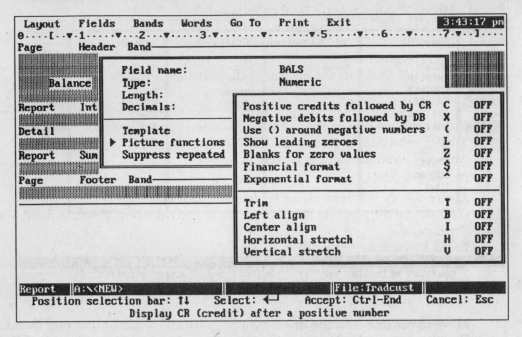

Figure 5.4

We are going to alter the settings on the first 2 options 'Positive credits followed by CR' and 'Negative Credits followed by DB'.
Press the Space Bar or click mouse to change these settings to On.
This will clearly identify positive and negative customer balances.

Finally press the Ctrl-End keys twice to return to the Report Design screen.
You will now see the BALS field placed on the Detail Band as a number of 9's, representing the field length and type (9 = any numeric digit)

15. Move the cursor along the Detail Band and locate it directly under the first character of the word 'Surname' in the Page Header band.
Press the F5 key again.
This time select the SURNAME field, as above.
We do not want to alter the way that the surname appears in the report, so press Ctrl-End.
The SURNAME field should appear under the heading 'Surname' in the Header Band as a series of X's.
If it does not do the following to relocate it:

*Moving a Field*

Locate the cursor on the first character of the field.
Press F6 to select the field.
Use the right arrow key to highlight the whole field. Press Return.
Press F7 to select Move.
Now move the cursor to the new starting position for the field.
Press Return again.

> Mouse users – move a field as follows:
> Click the field to highlight it.
> Click 'Select F6' at the bottom of the screen.
> Press Return.
> Click 'F7 Move' at the bottom of the screen.
> Click the new position on the screen.

If the new position overlaps the old position you will get the message,
'Delete covered text and fields ? (Y/N)'.
Answer Y and the field is moved.

*Deleting a Field.*

Alternatively it can be easier to delete a field and then reselect it.
Delete a field by locating the cursor on it and selecting 'Remove field' from the
Fields menu.
Press F5 as before to reselect it

16. Now place the INITIALS and CUSTREF fields in the same way.
    You have now completed the report Detail Band.

17. *Totalling Columns.*

    Move the cursor to the shaded area beneath the Report Summary Band.
    This band is printed at the end of the report, and can be used to display final
    totals. We are going to total the BALS field to produce the total owed to the
    company. Locate the cursor in column 5, i.e. underneath where BALS appears in
    the Detail Band.

18. Press F5 and move the cursor to the 4th column of the Add a Field menu.
    Select the SUM function – see figure 5.3.
    A specification window appears.
    Select the fourth option, 'Field to summarise on'.
    A field list appears. Select BALS.
    Now select the 'Picture functions' menu choice and set these 2 options to ON:
    'Positive credits followed by CR' and 'Negative Credits followed by DB'.

19. Finally press Ctrl-End twice to place the Summed field on the Summary Band.

20. *Printing the Report.*
    We have now finished designing the report, and will preview it on the screen
    before printing.
    Open the Print menu at the top of the screen and select the option 'View report on
    screen'.
    After a minute or so to compile, the report will be displayed – see Figure 5.1.
    Press Esc, followed by Return, to return to the Report Design screen.

21. Now use F10 to open the Layout menu.
    Select the option 'Edit description of report' and enter a suitable description.
    Make any amendments to the report if necessary, otherwise open the Exit menu
    and select 'Save Changes and Exit'.
    A 'save as' prompt appears, name the report CREDREP.
    After about two minutes to save the report, you are returned to the Control
    Center.

### Independent activities

Starting at the Control Center, select the report CREDREP in the Reports column.
Select the second option 'Modify layout' from the menu that appears.
Now make the following changes to the report:

1.  Move the cursor to the shaded area below the Report Summary band and add one blank line, and a centred end of listing message 'End of Report' i.e. 2 lines in all.

2.  Move to the shaded area below the Page Footer band, and using F5, add the page number from the list of predefined fields displayed.
    Centre the page number.

Try the following printing activities:

1.  Open the Print menu at the top of the screen and select the option, 'View Report on screen'.

2.  The dBASE IV report option offers a wide range of printing options; the following are included under the Print menu, and are supported by most printers.
    You may like to include them in your report:

    a.  'Eject page now' – ensures you begin your report on a new page.

    b.  'Output options' – offers sub-options allowing you to choose the number of copies and pages printed, and to alter the page numbering.

    c.  'Page dimensions' – allows you to alter the number of lines per page, and double or treble space records.

3.  If you are happy with the output from 1. above, then save the amended report.
    If you are connected to a printer select the 'Begin printing' option.

---

**Summary of commands used on forms design screen**

| | |
|---|---|
| *F5 key* | Selects fields to be used in report. |
| *F6 key* | Select a field on screen. |
| *F7 key* | Move a field on screen. |
| *F8 key* | Copy a field on screen. |
| *Ctrl-End keys* | Inserts a selected field into a report. |
| *Space Bar* | Toggles certain settings between on and off |

---

## Activity 3 *Creating and using a screen form*

### Objectives

1.  To create a data entry screen.
2.  To use the screen to add and amend records.

## Introduction

So far we have used the two standard DBASE IV screen formats for data entry and display – the Edit screen which displays individual records, and the Browse screen which displays records a screenful at a time.

However Edit and Browse may cause problems for inexperienced users – records may be accidentally changed or deleted, because there is no control over how the data is to be entered.

You have seen in the previous activity that a special report form can improve the appearance of printed reports. Similarly, designing your own screen forms can improve on the standard dBASE IV data entry screens.

Like a report, a form is based upon a database or view. Unlike a report it can also be used for input – to modify the records in the database.

When you create a screen, using the Forms Design screen, three files are created:

❒ the screen file with the extension . SCR

❒ a format file containing the underlying dBASE IV code – extension .FMT.

❒ a compiled version of the format file – extension .FMO.

A form is a special screen through which you can interact with a database file or view.

We are going to create a form or screen for the TRADCUST database. It will look like Figure 5.5.

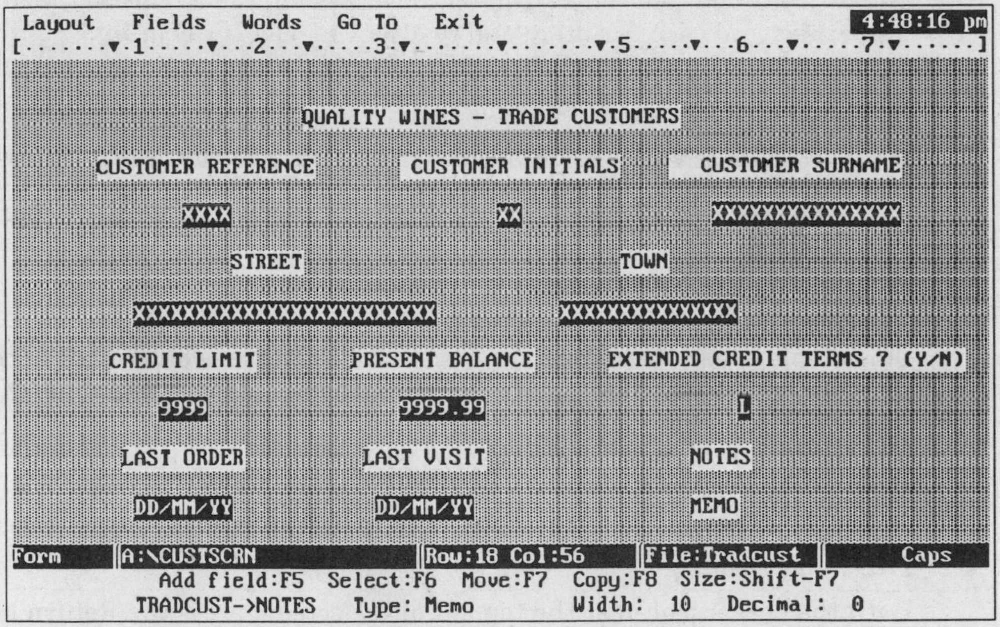

Figure 5.5

It is possible to use such screens in conjunction with programs, as we will see in later chapters.

**Guided activity**

1.  Starting from the Control Center, make sure that the TRADCUST database is open for use.
    Then move to the Forms column in the Control Center and select Create.

2.  The Forms Design screen appears – see Figure 5.6:

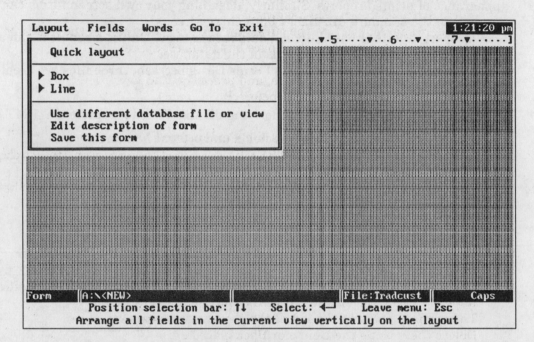

```
Layout    Fields    Words    Go To    Exit                        1:21:20 pm
                                      ·····▼·5····▼···6···▼·····7·▼······]
 ┌────────────────────────────────────┐
 │  Quick layout                       │
 │                                     │
 │ ▶ Box                               │
 │ ▶ Line                              │
 │                                     │
 │  Use different database file or view│
 │  Edit description of form           │
 │  Save this form                     │
 └────────────────────────────────────┘




Form    │A:\<NEW>                  │            │File:Tradcust│      Caps
          Position selection bar: ↑↓    Select: ↵    Leave menu: Esc
          Arrange all fields in the current view vertically on the layout
```

Figure 5.6

3.  The Layout menu should already be open.

    Select the option 'Quick layout'.
    This displays each field from the TRADCUST database on the left of the screen, together with the field templates showing the field length and type. (X = character, N = numeric etc.)
    Starting from this basic quick display we can:
    alter the layout of fields
    add text – titles and field headings remove unwanted fields draw boxes and lines.

4.  *Titles and Headings.*

    With the cursor placed at the top left of the screen, press the Return key twice.
    Two blank lines are inserted at the top of the screen.
    The Status Bar should read 'Row: 2 Col: 0'.

5.  Now type the screen title, QUALITY WINES – TRADE CUSTOMERS.
    Centre the heading as follows:
    Open the Words menu and select the Position option.
    Select 'Center' from the sub-menu that appears.
    The heading is now centered.

6. Next make sure that the Ins key is on. (check status bar)
Press the End key to move to the end of the line, and press Return twice to insert two more blank lines.
The status line should confirm that you are at row 4, col 0. We will now insert the field headings.
Type the first three as follows:

Customer Reference   Customer Initials   Customer Surname

To achieve a balanced layout (see Figure 5.5. above) you may need to insert or delete spaces between the headings:
To insert spaces, position the cursor on the first character of the heading.
Then use the Ins key and the Space bar to insert spaces,
To delete spaces use the delete key.
Centre these headings as before, and press the End key.
Insert two more blank lines as before.

7. *Moving the Fields.*

We now want to place the three fields under these headings.
Locate the cursor on the CUSTREF field (i.e. on the field template not the field name).
The field name and description are confirmed under the status bar at the bottom of the screen.
Press F6, followed by Return, to select the field.
Press F7 to begin moving it.
Use the arrow keys to reposition the field under the heading 'Customer Reference'.
Press Return to complete the move. The field now moves to its new position.
Repeat these steps for the INITIALS and SURNAME fields.
The original fields on the left of the screen are no longer needed.
Delete them using the Delete or Backspace key.

8. Now complete the rest of the fields and headings, as shown in Figure 5.5. The three steps are:

   a. type headings. (see section 6)

   b. position field under heading. (see section 7)

   c. delete original field name. (see section 7)

You will find that if you continue to leave a blank line between headings and fields you will be able to fit them all on one screen.
However, if you make a mistake, the following keys and commands can be used:
*Alterations and Corrections.*

Remove a field – locate cursor on field, then press the Delete key
Add a field – Press F5, select field, then Ctrl-End
Remove a line – Locate the cursor on the line. Select 'Remove line' option from the Words menu.

9. *Drawing Boxes.*
When the screen is fully defined, open the layout menu,and select the Box option.
Select Double line from the sub-menu that appears.
A message appears at the bottom of the screen.

Locate the cursor at the top left of the screen and press Return. This defines the upper left corner of the box.
Press the down arrow key to draw the left side of the box.
When you reach row 19, press the right arrow to draw the rest of the box.
Continue until the box encloses all the text on screen, then press Return to finish the box.

10. If you make a mistake delete the box as follows:
Locate the cursor on the box.
Press the Delete key.

11. We have now created the screen, open the Layout menu and select the option 'Edit description of form'.
A description box appears, enter the description, 'Data entry screen for the TRADCUST database'.
Next open the Exit menu and take the option 'Save changes and exit'.
Save the screen as CUSTSCRN when you are prompted. The screen will take some time to compile.
You will be returned to the Control Center. CUSTSCRN is listed in the Forms column.
When highlighted the description appears at the bottom of the screen.

## Independent activities

Starting from the Control Center, select the CUSTSCRN form and then select the 'Display data' option.
The screen form will be displayed; Press F10 to open the menu bar.
If you find that the screen overlaps the menu bar, return to Screen Design to change it – see next activity.
Use the Records menu to add a new customer living in Dorchester – supply the rest of the details yourself.
To open the memo field, locate the cursor on the field and press F9.

Mouse users – double click on memo field.

To exit and save the memo field press Ctrl-End.
Now use the Go to menu to go to the first record in the database.
Amend the last visit date to the 13th June.
Finally exit and save these changes.

---

**Summary of commands used**

(In the Forms Design Screen)

| | |
|---|---|
| *F5* | Add a field (With cursor located on field) |
| *F6* | Select a field |
| *F7* | Move a field |
| *Delete* | Delete field |

---

# Activity 4 *Controlling user input – data validation*

### Objectives

1. To modify a screen entry form.
2. To edit screen fields to control user input.

### Introduction

The screen form CUSTSCRN offers a better layout than the standard dBASE Edit and Browse screens.

However we still need to prevent an inexperienced user from entering incorrect data into the fields, and causing errors in the TRADCUST database.

### Guided activity

1. Starting at the Control Center, select the CUSTSCRN form, then select the option 'Modify layout'.

2. The Forms Design screen appears – check the Status Bar at the bottom of the screen. The TRADCUST database has been opened automatically.
   *Note*: Make sure that the Ins key is off during this Activity.

3. First we will ensure that the customer reference field is entered correctly.
   The correct format is 1 alphabetic character, followed by 3 numeric characters – i.e. numbers or digits.
   At the moment the format is XXXX which allows anything to be entered.
   Move the cursor on to the CUSTREF field template (i.e. the field not the heading) and press F5.
   The Modify Field Template window appears – see Figure 5.7.

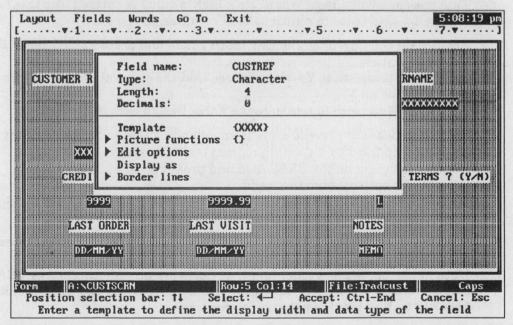

Figure 5.7

95

Press Return to select the Template option, and a list of character template symbols appear. They are summarised at the end of this activity.

Delete the 4 X's using the Backspace or Delete keys.

Now we will insert our own template. Insert an A, (representing any Alphabetic character) followed by three 9's (representing any numeric digit)

The template now shows A999 – press Return.

4.  We will now ensure that the first letter of the field is entered in upper case. (this simplifies searching)

    Now select the second option – 'Picture functions'

    A sub-menu appears – highlight the second option, 'Upper case conversion', and press the Space Bar or use the mouse to set it to ON.

    Now press Ctrl-End to save this setting and close the sub-menu.

    Press Ctrl-End again to return to the Form Design screen.

5.  Using the above steps:

    a.  use the Template option to insert A's instead of X's into the templates of the INITIALS, SURNAME AND TOWN fields.

    b.  edit the INITIALS, SURNAME, STREET and TOWN fields to upper case conversion.

6.  The maximum credit limit for a trade customer is £5,000.

    Move the cursor on the CREDLIM field and press F5.

    Select the 'Edit options' from the window, and then select the 'Largest allowed value' option from the submenu that appears.

    Insert 5000 and press Return.

    Now select the 'Unaccepted Message' option from the submenu.

    Type the message 'Credit Limit Cannot Exceed £5000'.

    This message will appear whenever a higher value is entered into this field.

    Press Ctrl-End twice to return to the Form Design screen.

7.  Now locate the Cursor on the EXCREDIT field and press F5 and select the Template option.

    Amend the template to Y – this ensures that the only valid input to this logical field is a Y or an N.

    Press Ctrl-End twice to return to the Form Design Screen.

8.  Finally we want to prevent users from amending the customer's current balance. (It will be updated by a special program – see Chapter 8.)

    Locate the cursor on the BALS field and press F5.

    Select 'Edit options' from the menu.

    Highlight the option 'Editing allowed' from the sub-menu and use the Space Bar to set it to No. Use Ctrl-End to return to the Form Design screen.

9.  We have now completed our editing of the data entry fields on the screen form CUSTREF.

    Date fields, i.e. the last order and visit dates are already checked by dBASE for correct format – British in our case – and do not require any further editing.

    Use F10 to Exit and Save these modifications.

### Independent activities

1. Use CUSTSCRN to enter another new record for a Dorchester customer and check that the data validation procedures work correctly, i.e. spaces not allowed. Only numbers and digits can be entered where appropriate. The balance field cannot be amended.
   The Credit limit cannot exceed £5000.

2. Design your own screen form ADDCHECK to change customers' addresses. Incorporate the following:

   > Title and field headings
   > Only the 4 fields holding name and address – delete the rest

   > Editing of fields to convert data entered to upper case

   > Run and test this screen form.

---

### Summary of template symbols

| Symbol | Field accepts only: |
|---|---|
| 9 | numeric digits and signs (+ – * /) |
| # | numeric digits, signs, spaces and periods |
| A | alphabetic characters only |
| N | numeric digits, alphabetic characters, and underscore (_) |
| X | any character |
| L | (logical fields only) Y,N,T or F |
| Y | (logical fields only) T or F only |
| ! | converts text entered to upper case |

---

## Activity 5 *Using the application generator*

### Objectives

1. To use the dBASE IV Application Generator.

2. To produce a quick application.

### Introduction

So far we have created a customer database and used the Control Center to retrieve, display and organise the records. We have also learnt how to create printed reports and screen forms. These are some of the building blocks of a complete system for running the customer database. What we need now is to link them all together into a user application by means of a main menu. Then users would only need to select a menu option such as 'Add a Customer Record' and they would be taken straight to your customised screen form.

This would be much simpler for inexperienced users than learning to use the Control Center as you have done.

You can create a user main menu by writing a program, as we will see in later chapters, but we can also do it more simply by using the dBASE IV applications generator.

In this activity we will generate a quick application with standard menu options.

**Guided activity**

1. Starting from the Control Center, select Create in the Applications column. Select 'Application Generator' from the box that appears next, and you are taken into the Application Definition screen – see Figure 5.8.

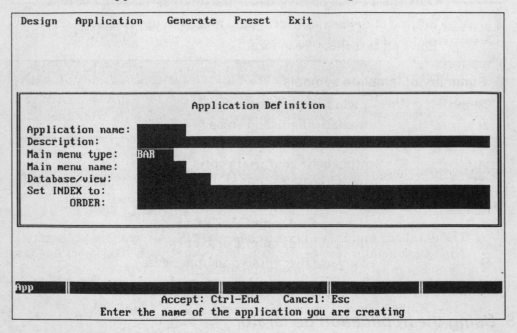

Figure 5.8

2. Complete the screen as follows:

    Application name: CUSQUICK

    Description: Quick application for customer database

    Main menu type: BAR (i.e. accept default)

    Main menu name: MAINMENU

    Database/view: TRADCUST.DBF

    Set index to: TRADCUST.MDX Order: CUSNAME.

We have thus named and described our application, chosen the type of menu – a bar menu displays in horizontal bars – and defined the database and index files that the main menu will use.

i.e our main menu will be used to gain access to the TRADCUST database, and uses an index file CUSNAME to retrieve the records in customer surname order.

Press Ctrl– End to save these choices.

3. The Application Generator Desktop appears next.
Ignore the black 'Application Object' box in the middle of the screen, and open the Application menu.
Then select the option 'Generate quick application'.
A further dialogue box appears next – see Figure 5.9.

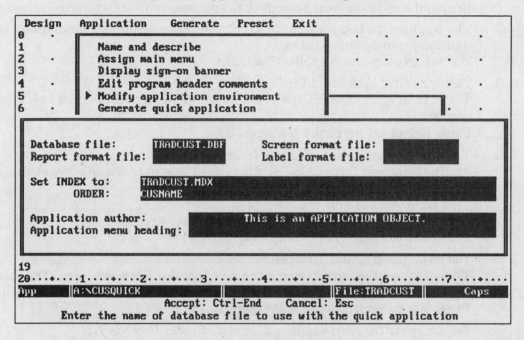

Figure 5.9

The database and index names chosen previously are already inserted.
The Quick Application Generator allows you to select a report file, a screen form file and a label file in its menu of applications.

4. Move to the entry box for the screen format file.
Press Shift-F1 to display a list of screen files.
Select CUSTSCRN.

5. Repeat these steps to select CREDREP as the Report format file.

6. Now move the cursor to the Application Menu Heading box.
Insert the menu title 'Quality Wines – Trade Customers'.

7. We have now defined our quick application.
Press Ctrl-End to save it.
Select Yes in the prompt box that appears.
The Application Generator takes a minute or so to produce a program of about 600 lines – CUSQUICK.PRG.

8. When prompted press any key to continue, then press Esc to close the Application menu.
Now open the Exit menu, then save changes and exit.

9. You are returned to the Control Center. Notice that CUSQUICK is shown in the Applications column.

**Independent activities**

1.   Starting from the Control Center, select the application CUSQUICK.
     Select 'Run application' from the box that appears.
     Respond Yes to the next prompt that appears.

2.   The application takes a minute to compile, then displays a main menu of key
     database management tasks.
     We will explore these application tasks.

3.   Take the first option: Add Information.
     The screen form CUSTSCRN is displayed allowing you to add a new customer
     record.
     Press Esc to return to the main menu.

4.   Take the second option: Change Information.
     Again the screen form CUSTSCRN is used as a user-friendly 'front end' to the
     database.
     This time you can edit records.
     Use the PgUp and PgDn keys to select different records.
     Press Esc to return to the main menu.

5.   Take the third option: Browse.
     This displays the records using the now familiar Browse screen. Try this option.
     Notice that they are displayed in the order of the selected index file – CUSNAME.
     Press Esc to return to the main menu.

6.   *Do not select the fourth option, Discard Marked Records yet!*

     Although included as standard by the Application Generator, it will permanently
     remove any records that you may have marked for deletion – see Chapter 4.
     First use the third option to unmark all records, then try this option.

7.   The fifth option, Print Report, will automatically print the report file that you
     selected, CREDREP.

8.   The sixth option, Reindex Databases will update all indexes held in the index file
     TRADCUST.MDX.
     You should do this if you have added or changed any records using options 1– 3.

9.   When you have experimented with the main menu options in this application,
     choose the final option to return to the Control Center.

# Section 3

# Commands & programming – dBASE III & dBASE IV

Once you leave the menu-driven part of dBASE and start to use the dot prompt or to program, the commands used are virtually identical, whichever version of dBASE you are using.

Instructions applying to both dBASE III and dBASE IV are in ordinary typeface, instructions specific to one version but not the other appear in italics.

'dBASE' is used to refer to either dBASE III or dBASE IV.

# Chapter 6

# Entering commands at the dot prompt

**Introduction to chapter**

*All our activities so far have used menus.*
*In dBASE III+ the menu-driven mode is known as the Assist, in dBASE IV the Control Center; it offers a powerful, easy interface for those starting dBASE. However, as we saw briefly in Chapters 1 and 3, another way of using dBASE exists. Instead of selecting commands from menus, you can type them directly on the screen using a command line called the 'dot prompt'.*

*Both methods have their advantages:*
*Using the Assist or Control Center reduces learning time and memory load, especially in early stages.*
*Issuing commands at the dot prompt seems fiddly and difficult at first, but in some cases may be easier than following a complex route through a series of menus. The commands, whichever mode you use, are logically equivalent, so identical results will be achieved.*

*In this chapter you will be learning the dot prompt equivalents of menu choices. In many cases a single command, e.g. CREATE SCREEN, will take you to the same design screen that you have already used in earlier chapters.*
*Our activities will be based on a new database TRADTRAN, which will hold the transactions for the TRADCUST database.*

## The syntax of dot prompt commands

To use commands effectively you must understand their syntax or logical layout.

Commands can consist of the following 4 parts:

1. *Verb* – the command itself, telling the system to do something, e.g. LIST, BROWSE, EDIT, USE

2. *Scope* – this is optional and can be used to restrict the command to part of the database, e.g. NEXT 20
   We will not be using it for the small databases that we are working with.

3. *Expression List* – this is usually optional, and is often used to stipulate which database or fields to include. e.g.
   USE TRADCUST
   LIST SURNAME, INITIALS, LASTORD

4.  *Conditions* – these are also optional; there are two main conditions,

    a.   FOR  e.g. LIST FOR SURNAME = 'WILSON'

    b.   WHILE  e.g. WHILE BALS > 2000

Only the verb – the command itself – is always compulsory.

The commands used will be listed at the end of each activity, as before.

*Conventions used:*

Commands are shown in upper case for clarity, but may be typed in either upper or lower. The exceptions are variables or field values included in the command.

So, e.g. LIST FOR SURNAME = 'WILSON' would not retrieve 'Wilson'.

When you see an item in angle brackets e.g., DISPLAY < field list >, substitute your own value, e.g. DISPLAY SURNAME, INITIALS. Do not type the brackets.

Items enclosed in Square brackets [ ] are optional  e.g. LIST [TO PRINTER]. Do not type the brackets.

A command must always be followed by pressing the Return key.

I shall assume that you know this from now on.

# Activity 1 *Using the dot prompt*

## Objectives

1.  To move between the Menu-Driven and dot prompt modes.

2.  To set the default drive and directory.

3.  To use the Help facility.

4.  To enter and recall commands at the dot prompt.

5.  To exit from dBASE using the dot prompt.

## Introduction

In this quick guided tour of the dot prompt we shall be finding out some of its basic features.

## Guided activity

1.  dBASE III PLUS USERS *only*.  Starting from the Assist screen, press Esc.

    dBASE IV USERS *only*.  Starting at the Control Center, press Esc, then type Y to the prompt asking you if you want to abandon the operation.

You are now taken to the dot prompt screen. At the bottom of the screen is the status bar.

A single full stop – the dot prompt – appears bottom left, just above the status bar.

If your system has been set up to show a slightly different prompt, don't worry.

2. Press the F2 key and you are returned to the Menu screen.
   Return the dot prompt again using the Esc key.
   Type ASSIST at the dot prompt and press Return – this has the same effect as F2.
   Return to the dot prompt again.

3. *Setting the Drive.*

   If you are using a work disk in drive A, then you must remember to reset the default drive whenever you first enter dBASE, otherwise your work will be saved onto C drive.
   The command is SET DEFAULT TO < DRIVE >
   Type SET DEFAULT TO A: if you wish to change drives.
   The status bar will now show A:

4. *Using Help.*

   Press the F1 key to call the Help facility.
   Select the first option, Commands, from the Table of Contents that appears.
   A list of dBASE commands appears. You will find them a valuable source of reference.
   Press Esc to exit Help.

5. *Opening Databases.*

   We will try issuing a few commands now.
   Type USE TRADCUST
   The status bar confirms that the correct database and drive are in use.
   Notice that when the database is first opened the record pointer is set to the first record – 1/17 (your database may have less or more records than this)

6. *Recalling Commands.*

   Now type the command LIST.
   Next type the command DISPLAY ALL.
   The two commands are fairly similar.
   Now let's repeat these commands – press the up arrow key once.
   The last command – DISPLAY ALL is recalled, press Return to execute it.
   Now keep pressing the up arrow key and all your previous commands are recalled.
   Press the down arrow key until you recall the LIST command.
   Press Return to execute it.
   The dBASE 'history buffer' normally stores up to 20 commands which can then be recalled, amended if necessary using the Delete and Insert keys, and re-issued.
   This is useful as it saves re-keying complex commands. If it doesn't work, then your system has been set up differently.
   If so type the commands,

   SET HISTORY ON (+ Return)

   SET HISTORY TO 20 (+ Return)

   and try this section again.

7. Issue the command DISPLAY STRUCTURE.

The name, drive, number of records, update date, and field descriptions for the active database are listed.

8. *Command Abbreviation.*

   Shorten this command to DISP STRU – it works just the same.
   All dBASE command verbs can be shortened to the first four letters of each words (but not field names, file names, or variable names).

9. *Closing Databases.*

   Databases should be closed as soon as you have finished with them, otherwise they could be accidentally corrupted, e.g. through a power failure.
   Type CLOSE DATABASES (or CLOS DATA)

10. *Quitting dBASE.*

    You must exit from dBASE properly – simply turning off the machine can also damage your files.
    Type QUIT to exit from dBASE.

## Independent activities

1. Starting at the Assist/Control Center, change to the dot prompt.

2. Change the default drive/directory if necessary.

3. Open the TRADCUST database.

4. Issue the command LIST, then the command DISPLAY ALL.

   What is the difference between them?

5. Look them up in Help.

6. Close the TRADCUST database and quit from dBASE.

| Summary of commands used | |
|---|---|
| *Esc* | Go to dot prompt from Assist/Control Center |
| *F2 or ASSIST* | Return to the Assist/Control Center from the dot prompt |
| *F1* | Help |
| *SET DEFAULT TO <DRIVE>* | Select the drive |
| *USE <FILENAME>* | Open a database file for use |
| *LIST* | Display all records in the current database |
| *DISPLAY ALL* | As LIST, but a screenful at a time |
| *SET HISTORY ON* | Allows issued commands to be saved |
| *SET HISTORY TO <N>* | Specifies the maximum number of previously issued commands to be saved |

| | |
|---|---|
| *Up arrow* | Recalls previous dot prompt commands |
| *DISPLAY STRUCTURE* | Displays current database structure |
| *CLOSE DATABASES* | Closes all databases in use |
| *QUIT* | Exit from dBASE |

## Activity 2 *Creating and searching a database*

### Objectives

1. To create a database using the dot prompt.
2. To add records using the dot prompt.
3. To take a backup copy of a database using the dot prompt.
4. To display the structure of a database.

### Introduction

In the next few activities we will be working with a new database – TRADTRAN.DBF. This database will hold details of Quality Wines payments from their trade customers – the clubs, off-licenses and restaurants that they supply with wine.
The database has the following structure:

| FIELDNAME | TYPE | WIDTH | COMMENTS |
|---|---|---|---|
| CUSTREF | Char | 4 | format T001, T002 etc. |
| CUSTYPE | Char | 1 | C = Club, O = Off-license R = Restaurant |
| ORDERDAT | Date | 8 | Date of Customer Order |
| VALUE | Num | 7.2 | Value of Order |
| ORDNO | Char | 5 | Order Number |

Every trade customer has a unique reference number – CUSTREF – which is also held on the TRADCUST database.
In later activities we shall use this common field to update the TRADCUST database.

### Guided activity

1. Starting from the dot prompt, make sure that you are using the correct drive.
   If necessary set the date to UK format using the command,
   SET DATE BRITISH
   Type the command CREATE TRADTRAN.
   The database design screen appears that you used previously to create the TRADCUST database.

The drive and database name are confirmed in the status bar.
Enter the structure for the 5 fields shown above in the introduction.

*dBASE USERS* III          refer to Section 1 Chapter 1, for guidance.

*dBASE USERS* IV           refer to Section 2 Chapter 3, for guidance.    *P 51*

Notes:

a.   *dBASE USERS* IV *only.*          Enter an N in the index column of each field.

b.   When you select date as the field type for ORDERDAT, the width of 8 is
     automatically allocated.

2.   After you have completed the final field press Return twice and a message asks
     you to confirm the end of the operation.
     Press Return again, answer N to the question, 'Input data records now? (Y/N)'.
     You are returned to the dot prompt.
     Note that the database is still open.

3.   We will now add the following 6 records to the database:

| CUSTREF | CUSTYPE | ORDERDAT | VALUE | ORDNO |
|---------|---------|----------|-------|-------|
| T001 | C | 27/02/92 | 250.00 | S1430 |
| T002 | C | 26/07/92 | 100.50 | S1444 |
| T003 | O | 28/07/92 | 234.58 | S1450 |
| T006 | R | 29/07/92 | 75.00 | S1472 |
| T002 | C | 03/08/92 | 220.00 | S1488 |
| T003 | O | 02/08/92 | 46.00 | S1500 |

4.   Type APPEND.
     Enter the 6 records exactly as shown above – make sure that you use upper case
     throughout, and distinguish the letter O from the digit 0.
     When finished, press Ctrl-End to exit and return to the dot prompt.

5.   Let's check our 6 records:
     Type BROWSE at the dot prompt.
     The Browse screen is displayed, check that your records are all correct.
     Exit to the dot prompt.

6.   Type LIST – the records are listed.
     If you are connected to a printer try the command,
     LIST TO PRINTER (or LIST TO PRINT)

7.   Close the database and quit from dBASE.

**Independent activity**

It is essential that the definition of the CUSTREF field is the same in both the TRADTRAN and the TRADCUST databases, and that the common field CUSTREF references the same customer.

Do the following to make sure:

1.  At the dot prompt, check your default drive.

2.  Open TRADCUST and browse it.

    Ensure that you still have the following 4 customers:

    | CUSTREF | SURNAME | INITIAL | ETC. |
    |---------|---------|---------|------|
    | T001 | FRANKS | | |
    | T002 | SMITH | JB | |
    | T003 | HARRIS | | |
    | T006 | PATEL | | |

    If not amend the records. Be sure not to confuse the digit 0 with the letter O. Exit TRADCUST to the dot prompt.

3.  Using the USE command, open TRADTRAN and check that the customer reference numbers are as in Figure 6.1.
    If so they match the ones held in the TRADCUST database.

4.  Finally open each database in turn and display their structure using the command DISPLAY STRUCTURE or DISP STRU.
    You may add the parameter TO PRINTER if you have one.

5.  As mentioned previously, it is good policy to make regular backup copies of essential business data, to guard against accidental loss or damage.

    Open the TRADTRAN database and issue the command: COPY TO TRADTRBK
    A message appears confirming the number of records copied.
    Repeat for the TRADCUST database – COPY TO TRADCUBK.
    For additional security a copy can be made to C drive. The command would be:
    COPY TO C:TRADTRBK
    A confirmation message appears again. An unwanted copy can be erased using the ERASE command – the file extension e.g. DBF must be included.

    *Great care must be taken with the ERASE command, otherwise the wrong files may be accidentally deleted.*

6.  Issue the command DIR – this displays the databases on your drive.
    Issue the command DIR *.* – this lists all files on your drive.
    Issue the command dir *.BAK – this displays the backup versions of your databases that dBASE takes automatically.

7.  Close the databases and quit dBASE.

---

**Summary of commands used**

| Command | Description |
|---|---|
| CREATE <database name> | Creates a new database file |
| APPEND † | Adds records to end of database |
| BROWSE † | Displays records (may be edited) |
| LIST [TO PRINTER] † | Lists all fields [to printer] (no editing possible) |
| COPY TO <file name.ext> † | Makes copy of database under another name |
| ERASE <file name.ext> | Erases a file permanently |
| DIR | Lists all databases on disk |
| DIR *.* | Lists all files on disk |
| DIR *.<ext> | Lists all files with stated extension |
| SET DATE BRITISH | Sets date to UK format |

† require that a database is in use

---

## Activity 3 *Displaying, modifying and ordering the database*

### Objectives

1. To modify the structure of the TRADTRAN database.
2. To position the record pointer.
3. To display selected records and selected fields.
4. To retrieve selected records for amendment.
5. To mark selected records for deletion.
6. To perform arithmetic operations – SUM, AVERAGE, and COUNT.
7. To index and sort the database.

### Introduction

We have already achieved all the above objectives using the Assist or Control Center. This activity briefly teaches you the same skills at the dot prompt.

### Guided activity

1. From the dot prompt, open the TRADTRAN database.
2. *Modifying the database structure.*

   We are going to add a logical field POSTED.
   Initially it will be set to N.
   TRADTRAN is a transaction file – it stores details of order dates and balances, which will be used to update the customer master file – TRADCUST.

After the transactions are added (or posted) to the customer's balance the POSTED field can be set to Y.

Issue the command MODIFY STRUCTURE (MODI STRU).

Add the 6th field POSTED to the end of the database – define it as a logical field.

dBASE IV USERS      enter an N in the index column.

Exit and save the new structure.

3. *Amending Records.*

   Issue the BROWSE or EDIT command.
   Enter N in the POSTED field for the 6 records.
   Exit and save.
   Use LIST to confirm the changes to the 6 records.

4. We should now take a backup copy to save these changes.
   Issue the command, COPY TO TRADTRBK.
   You are warned that this will overwrite the previous version of TRADTRBK.
   Select the Overwrite option.
   Open TRADTRBK and list its contents – it should be identical to TRADTRAN.

5. *Displaying and listing records.*

   Open TRADTRAN again (this automatically closes the TRADTRBK database).
   LIST and DISPLAY, used without any additional parameters, behave differently.
   Type LIST. The complete database is displayed.
   Type DISPLAY. No record is displayed.
   This is because the command DISPLAY only displays the current record.

   At the moment the status bar shows that the current record is EOF or end of file, so no record is current.
   Issue the command GO TOP. The record pointer is now set to record 1 – see status bar.
   Re-issue the DISPLAY command.
   Record 1 is displayed – the current record.
   Issue the command GO BOTTOM.
   The pointer is set to the last record. Type DISPLAY ALL. The complete database is displayed.
   DISPLAY ALL has the advantage with larger databases of pausing as each screenful of records is displayed – unlike LIST.

6. *Displaying selected fields.*

   Often we only wish to select certain fields in the database for retrieval.
   This is simple using LIST or DISPLAY ALL.
   Type LIST CUSTREF, CUSTYPE, ORDERDAT
   These three fields are displayed.
   Use the up arrow to recall this command, and then use the Ins and Delete keys to amend it to:

   LIST CUSTREF, VALUE, ORDERDAT

| Mouse users – may click anywhere on the command line to delete or insert.

Issue this command.

7. *Displaying selected records – searching character fields.*

Suppose that we wish to list only transactions for type C customers.

Issue the command, LIST FOR CUSTYPE = 'C'
Three records are displayed. CUSTYPE is the field searched, and 'C' is the search term.
Characters need enclosing in single or double quotes.
Recall the command and amend the search term 'C' to lower case - 'c'
Re-issue the command and no records are retrieved. Cases must match when searching character fields.

Issue the command LIST FOR CUSTREF = 'T003'.
Two records are retrieved and displayed.

8. *Displaying selected records – searching numeric and date fields.*

When searching numeric or date fields the following operators can be used:

> greater than
< less than
<> not equal to
= equal to
>= greater than or equal to
<= less than or equal to

Issue the command, LIST FOR VALUE = 250.
This displays the one customer transaction for £250.
Experiment with re-issuing this command, using a different operator each time.
Different sets of records are displayed.

*Date fields –* $\overset{\curvearrowleft}{\underset{d}{\text{BASE USERS}}}$ III

Dates need converting to be used as search conditions.
Issue the command: LIST FOR ORDERDAT >CTOD('31/07/92')
This lists all transactions for August onwards.

*Date fields –* $\overset{\curvearrowleft}{\underset{d}{\text{BASE USERS}}}$ IV

Dates need enclosing in curled brackets to be used as search conditions. Issue the command: LIST FOR ORDERDAT > {31/07/92}

This lists all transactions for August onwards.

9.  We can now combine activities 7 and 8 above – displaying certain fields of certain records.
    The syntax of the command is: LIST [<FIELD LIST>] [ FOR <CONDITIONS>]

    III Issue the command:

    LIST CUSTREF, ORDERDAT, VALUE FOR ORDERDAT >CTOD('31/07/92')

    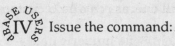IV Issue the command:

    LIST CUSTREF, ORDERDAT, VALUE FOR ORDERDAT > {31/07/92}

    Three fields of two records are displayed.

10. *AND. and .OR.*

    Suppose that we want to retrieve transactions for both R and C type customers.
    This requires the logical connector 'or'.
    Don't confuse 'or' with 'and' – a common mistake.
    We want to retrieve records where the CUSTYPE field contains either R or C – not both!
    Issue the command: LIST FOR CUSTYPE = 'C' .OR. CUSTYPE = 'R'
    Records fulfilling either condition are listed. (Note: logical connectors .AND. .OR. and .NOT. must start and end with a full stop)

    'And' on the other hand requires that both conditions be present, and is often used to test conditions in 2 fields.
    Issue the command: LIST FOR CUSTYPE = 'C' .AND. .NOT. POSTED
    Transactions are listed only if the customer type is C and the transaction has not been posted.

    Note:   a.   the use of the logical operator .NOT.
            b.   how to use a logical field as a condition – you don't type POSTED = 'N' but .NOT. POSTED.

11. *Deleting and recalling records.*

    The syntax of the DELETE command resembles that of the LIST command – except that no field list is required.
    Recall the previous command and amend it to:
    DELETE FOR CUSTYPE = 'C' .AND. .NOT. POSTED
    A message '3 records deleted' appears.
    Type BROWSE. Use the arrow keys to select each of the 6 records in turn, and observe the status bar.
    'Del' appears in the status bar for the 3 records marked for deletion.
    Select record 6, and press Esc to return to the dot prompt.
    Type RECALL. A message 'No records recalled' appears.
    This is because RECALL is similar to DISPLAY – it only operates on the current record.

As record 6 was not marked for deletion, it was not recalled.
Type RECALL ALL. The message '3 records recalled' appears.
BROWSE to confirm that they have been unmarked.

12. *Arithmetic commands, SUM, COUNT and AVERAGE.*

Used with numeric fields, their syntax resembles the LIST command, i.e. :

            \<COMMAND> [\<FIELD LIST>] [ FOR \<CONDITIONS>]

Used without any parameters they will operate on all the numeric fields in the database.
In the TRADTRAN database there is only one numeric field – VALUE, holding the value of each transaction.

Try the following:

    Type SUM – The value of all transactions is summed and listed.

    Type AVERAGE – The average value of all transactions is listed.

    Type COUNT – The number of records in the database is displayed.

It is also possible to use these commands with conditions,

    Type COUNT FOR CUSTREF = 'T002'
    This counts the number of transactions for customer reference T002.

13. *Global replacement – the REPLACE command.*

Sometimes it is useful to replace values held in a number of records in one operation – global replacement.
e.g. if a batch of orders have been posted to the customer account then the POSTED field in all the batch can be set to .T.
Issue the command: REPLACE ALL POSTED WITH .T.
List the database to check that this global change has been made.

14. *Re-ordering records – sorting.*

As you will remember from previous activities, sorting the database creates a new database with the records sorted into a new order.
Its disadvantage is that it needs resorting every time records are added or amended.

We will create a new database sorted in order number sequence.
Issue the command, SORT ON ORDNO TO ORDTRAN
A message confirms its creation.
Open this new database and list it to confirm the new sorted order.

Open the TRADTRAN database again.

*Sections 15 and 16 apply to dBASE III only.*

*dbase IV users skip to section 17 and 18.*

15. *Re-ordering records – indexing* **III** *BASE USERS*

Indexing a database, on the other hand, uses an index to display the records in a different order. Their original physical order remains unchanged.
Issue the command: INDEX ON CUSTREF TO REFDEX.
A message indicates when indexing is complete.

We have created an index file named REFDEX that displays the records in customer reference order – so all the transactions for the same customer are listed together.

This remains the active index until another is opened LIST the database and check this new order.

It is often useful to list customer transactions in order of their value.
Issue the command: INDEX ON VALUE TO VALUE
This new index VALUE becomes the active index, LIST the database in this new indexed order.

Finally let's create an index on more than one key.
It could be even more useful to list customer transactions in customer reference order and in order of their value.
i.e. CUSTREF is the primary key, and VALUE the secondary key. To combine key expressions of different types, VALUE must be converted to characters or a 'string' of text.
Issue the command: INDEX ON CUSTREF + STR(VALUE) TO REFVAL
This creates an index file called REFVAL.
LIST the database and check this new order.

16. *Using existing indexes* <sup>BASE USERS</sup> III

Any changes made to the records could affect their indexed order, e.g. changes to the VALUE or the BALANCE fields would affect the REFVAL and VALUE indexes.
All the different indexes need to be kept up to date.
Before you edit a key field in the database make sure that all the relevant indexes are open.
Issue the commands:
SET INDEX TO VALUE,REFVAL
BROWSE
Then amend the value for order number S1472 to 120.00
Exit and save.
Both indexes are open and will be reorganised.

*Sections 17 and 18 apply to dBASE IV only.*

*dbase III users skip to section 19.*

17. *Re-ordering records – indexing* <sup>BASE USERS</sup> IV

Indexing a database, on the other hand, uses an index to display the records in a different order. Their original physical order remains unchanged.
Issue the command: INDEX ON CUSTREF TAG REFDEX
A message indicates when indexing is complete. We have created an index tag named REFDEX that displays the records in customer reference order – so all the transactions for the same customer are listed together.
LIST the database and check this new order.

It is often useful to list CUSTOMER transactions in order of their value, largest transactions first.

However, the default order is ascending or smallest first.

Issue the command: INDEX ON VALUE TAG VALUE DESCENDING

This new index tag VALUE becomes the active index, LIST the database in this new indexed order.

Finally let's create an index on more than one key.

It could be even more useful to list customer transactions in customer reference order and in order of their value.

i.e. CUSTREF is the primary key, and VALUE the secondary key.

To combine key expressions of different types, VALUE must be converted to characters or a 'string' of text.

Issue the command: INDEX ON CUSTREF + STR(VALUE) TAG REFVAL

This creates an index tag called REFVAL.

LIST the database and check this new order.

18. *Using existing index tags*

All the different index tags are stored in a master index file, bearing the same name as the database, but having the extension .MDX

They are automatically updated to reflect changes in the database.

Issue the commands: SET ORDER TO TAG VALUE
LIST

The VALUE index is activated and LIST displays the database in this new order.

19. *Closing Indexes.*

Issue the command SET INDEX TO

This closes all indexes and restores the database to its natural (unindexed) order.

20. Finally close the database and quit dBASE.

## Independent activities

We will use the TRADCUST database for these activities.

1. Starting from the dot prompt, open the TRADCUST database for use.
   Display its structure (DISP STRU) to remind yourself of the fields.

2. List all the Poole customers.
   List all the customers called 'Smith' (remember to match upper case, where necessary)
   For clearer display, recall the two above commands, and list only the SURNAME, INITIALS, STREET and TOWN fields.
   If you have a printer add TO PRINTER to these commands.

3. It is possible to specify fields and conditions for editing too.
   Edit the record for customer PATEL using the command:
   EDIT FOR SURNAME = 'PATEL'
   Increase Patel's credit limit by £100 and save the change.

4. List the names and addresses for Poole and Bournemouth customers.
   Try both the .AND. and .OR. connectors.
   Try to work out why using .AND. will retrieve no customers.

5. Activate the NAMETOWN index and issue the above command again.
   What is the new order of the records?

6. Browse the TRADCUST database and make sure that no records are currently marked for deletion – if so then recall them.
   You should have one or two Dorchester customers. Issue the command to delete the records for Dorchester customers.

   You should get a deletion confirmation message –if not check spelling, capital letters, and use of quotes.

   We are now going to remove them permanently. Issue the command PACK. Two things happen:

   1. a message confirms that n number of records have been copied (original number minus deletions)

   2. (dBASE IV users *only*) the indexes are automatically rebuilt to take account of the

      deletions.

7. Add up the balances of all Poole customers. (TOWN = 'POOLE')
   Find the average balance of all customers.
   Count the number of Southampton customers.
   Find the average difference between the balance and credit limit fields.
   (BALS-CREDLIM)

8. Close the TRADCUST database using the command,
   CLOSE DATABASES and quit dBASE .

---

**Summary of commands used**

| | |
|---|---|
| *MODIFY STRUCTURE* | modify database structure |
| *GO TOP* | move record pointer to first record |
| *GO BOTTOM* | move record pointer to end of file |
| *DISPLAY* | display current record |
| *DISPLAY ALL* | display all records a screen at a time |
| *DELETE [ FOR <conditions>]* | marks records for deletion |
| *RECALL* | unmark current record marked for deletion |
| *RECALL ALL* | unmark all records marked for deletion |
| *PACK* | erase all records marked for deletion |
| *SORT ON <FIELD LIST> TO <FILE NAME>* | creates a sorted copy of a database |

dBASE III Users Only

| | |
|---|---|
| *INDEX ON <FIELD1 + FIELD2 ETC.> TO <FILENAME>* | creates an index file based on specified field(s) |
| *SET INDEX TO < INDEX FILE NAME >* | activates an index |
| *USE <FILENAME> INDEX <INDEX FILE NAME>* | opens a database in indexed order |

dBASE IV Users Only

| | |
|---|---|
| *INDEX ON <FIELD1 + FIELD2 ETC.> TAG <FILENAME> [<DESCENDING>]* | creates an index file based on specified field(s) (specify if DESCENDING required) |
| *SET ORDER TO TAG < INDEX FILE NAME >* | activates an index |
| *USE <FILENAME> ORDER TAG <INDEX FILE NAME>* | opens a database in indexed order. |

The following commands allow you to select certain fields using a field list, and certain records by specifying conditions.

| | |
|---|---|
| *EDIT [<FIELD LIST> FOR <CONDITIONS> ]* | edit record(s) |
| *LIST [<FIELD LIST> FOR <CONDITIONS> ]* | list record(s) |
| *COUNT [<FIELD LIST> FOR <CONDITIONS> ]* | count records |
| *SUM [<FIELD LIST> FOR <CONDITIONS> ]* | sum field(s) |
| *AVERAGE [<FIELD LIST> FOR <CONDITIONS> ]* | average field(s) |
| *REPLACE ALL <FIELDNAME> WITH <REPLACEMENT VALUE> FOR <CONDITIONS>* | replaces a field value with another value |

## Activity 4 *Creating screen forms and reports*

### Objectives

1. To design a data entry screen from the dot prompt.
2. To design a printed report from the dot prompt.

### Introduction

You will find that the dot prompt uses the same methods to design screens and printed reports as the Assist or the Control Center do.

In both cases, once you have issued the dot prompt command, you use the same design screens as before.

**Guided activity**

1. We are going to create a report based on the database that we have created – TRADTRAN.
   First open the database.
   Now create the report with the command: CREATE REPORT TRANREP

2. The Report Design screen will differ depending which version of dBASE you are using.

   *ᴮᴬˢᴱ ᵁˢᴱᴿˢ* III refer to Chapter 2, Activity 1.

   *ᴮᴬˢᴱ ᵁˢᴱᴿˢ* IV refer to Chapter 5, Activity 2.

   Pg. 84

   Design the report along the following lines:
   a. Title: 'Customer Order Transactions'
   b. Include all fields in the following order,
      CUSTREF, CUSTYPE, ORDNO, VALUE, ORDERDAT (double space them)
   c. Total the VALUE field.
   Save the report and exit to the dot prompt.

3. Make sure that the TRADTRAN database is open and that the index REFVAL is in use – see Activity 3.
   Now run the report using the command REPORT FORM TRANREP
   If you have a printer, add the parameter TO PRINT.
   If it needs modification, the command is: MODIFY REPORT TRANREP.

4. As a final activity, we will create a screen form for the TRADTRAN database.
   Starting from the dot prompt, ensure TRADTRAN is open for use.
   Then issue the command:
   CREATE SCREEN TRANSCRN
   You enter the Form Design Screen.

   *ᴮᴬˢᴱ ᵁˢᴱᴿˢ* III should refer to Chapter 2, Activity 2,

   *ᴮᴬˢᴱ ᵁˢᴱᴿˢ* IV should refer to Chapter 5, Activity 2. page 84

5. Design a data entry screen along the following lines:
   a. All fields can be edited.
   b. Use the Template, Edit options, and Picture functions to control input and display, e.g. :
      Upper case conversion
      Format checks on letters and numbers entered

119

6.  When you have designed and saved your screen form, open it for use with the command:  SET FORMAT TO TRANSCRN
    (The database it uses – TRADTRAN – must be open for use).
    Use the APPEND command and add a new record, testing the data validation checks that you have incorporated.
    If it needs modification, the command is:  MODIFY SCREEN TRANSCRN

**Independent activity**

The report TRANREP can be run using search conditions – see summary of commands below.

Issue the command to run the report for orders over £200.

---

**Summary of commands used**

| | |
|---|---|
| *CREATE REPORT < REPORT NAME >* | Create a report |
| *MODIFY REPORT < REPORT NAME >* | Modify a report |
| *REPORT FORM < REPORT NAME >*<br>*[ FOR <CONDITIONS> TO PRINTER ]* | Produce a report |
| *CREATE SCREEN < SCREEN NAME >* | Create a screen form |
| *MODIFY SCREEN < SCREEN NAME >* | Modify a screen form |
| *SET FORMAT TO < SCREEN NAME >* | Activate a screen form |

---

# Chapter 7

# An introduction to dBASE programming

## Introduction to the chapter

*dBASE can be used in four distinct modes. If you have worked through the previous sections, you have already encountered the first two or three :*

*ASSIST or CONTROL CENTER:*

*The series of pull down menus you see when you first enter dBASE.
In this mode the user chooses the appropriate commands from these menus.*

*THE APPLICATION GENERATOR (dBASE IV USERS only):*

*A powerful extension to the Control Center that enables you to link the databases, reports and screens by a series of user menus — in effect it generates a series of programs for you.*

*THE DOT PROMPT:*

*You are no longer supported by menus, instead you have to remember the commands yourself and enter them unassisted.
Daunting at first, but ultimately quicker and more powerful than using menus.*

*PROGRAMMING MODE:*

*When you use the dot prompt each command is executed as soon as Return is pressed, e.g. :*

*USE TRADCUST
LIST FOR TOWN = 'POOLE' .OR. TOWN = 'BOURNEMOUTH'*

*If you need to use these commands regularly they can be saved and re-used by storing them in a program file. The name of this file becomes the name of the program. The program can then be run as a batch of stored commands.
At its simplest then, a dBASE program is just a list of commands which could equally well have been issued individually at the dot prompt. However there are other more advanced commands and features which can only be used within programs.
Programming is not as difficult as you may think, if you can use the dot prompt you are already half way there!*

## Why learn to program?

Like the screen forms and the Application Generator, programming allows us to control user input.

In many commercial situations the individuals who design and control the database, e.g. programmers and analysts, are not the same people who will be entering the routine data on a day to day basis.

Management do not want, for example, data entry clerks being able to add, delete, or change records willy nilly.

By writing a program to, e.g. edit a customer record, a programmer can control the amount and type of data keyed in.

He can design the appearance of the screen and provide on-screen help and error handling. He can protect certain fields e.g. credit rating, from viewing and alteration.

None of these refinements are possible using the standard Edit and Browse screens, or dot prompt commands

## What is a Program?

A program is a series of instructions that tell the computer to carry out certain tasks.

To write these instructions in a form that the computer understands, you must use a special computer language – in this case the dBASE programming language.

A computer has no common sense or discretion and always follows your instructions to the letter – right or wrong! This means that even quite trivial programming errors will stop your program from working correctly.

When you start programming you will inevitably make a lot of these simple errors, e.g. misspelling, missing out spaces or commas.

Everybody goes through this learning stage so don't be disheartened!

## dBASE III and dBASE IV

*The programming commands used in this book are virtually identical for dBASE III or dBASE IV.*

Instructions applying to both are in ordinary typeface.

Instructions specific to dBASE III or IV only are marked with a special logo.

'dBASE' is used to refer to either dBASE III or IV.

*Conventions Used:*

In the following chapters on programming we shall be using the same conventions as before for describing the structure of commands :

Commands are shown in upper case for clarity, but may be typed in either upper or lower.

The exceptions are variables or field values included in the command.

So, e.g LIST FOR SURNAME = 'WILSON' would not retrieve 'Wilson'.

When you see an item in angle brackets e.g., DISPLAY < field list >, substitute your own value, e.g. DISPLAY SURNAME, INITIALS.

*Do not* type the brackets.

Items enclosed in Square brackets [ ] are optional.

e.g. LIST [TO PRINTER].

*Do not* type the brackets.

# Activity 1 *Creating, saving and running a program*

### Objectives

1. To create a simple program using the dBASE text editor
2. To save the program using a file name.

### Introduction

Our first program – CUSTADD1 – will call up the screen form CUSTSCRN and allow the user to add a new record.

```
*
* PROGRAM CUSTADD1.PRG
* < PROGRAMMER NAME AND CREATION/MODIFICATION DATE >
* CALLS TITLE SCREEN THEN SCREEN FORM CUSTSCRN
* ALLOWS USER TO APPEND NEW RECORD
*
?
?
SET DATE BRITISH
* DISPLAY COMPANY NAME AND CURRENT DATE
?'      QUALITY WINES        DATE:-   '+ DTOC(DATE())
?
?
?'        ADD A NEW TRADE CUSTOMER RECORD   '
?
?
WAIT
* OPEN DATABASE AND SCREEN ENTRY FORM
USE TRADCUST
SET FORMAT TO CUSTSCRN
APPEND BLANK
READ
CLOSE DATABASES
RETURN
```

*Explanation of the program.*

A line starting with an asterisk or star symbol * is a comment line.

Text after the * is ignored by the program; it reminds the programmer of the program's action and purpose.

123

At the start of the program always include program name, programmer name, date, and purpose of the program, as shown above.

Programs have to be maintained after they have been written – often by different members of a programming team, so readability is very important.

A line starting with a ? (question mark) symbol displays information on the screen on the first available line – called a row in dBASE terminology.

On its own the ? command inserts a blank line. Followed by a string of text in quotes, the ? command displays the text on screen.

So the program first displays two blank lines, then displays the text string,
' QUALITY WINES   DATE :'

The computer's current date is displayed next by using the DATE () function.

The DTOC () function is used to convert the date to characters – this is necessary so that it can be displayed on the same line as a string of text characters.

Whenever different data types are mixed on the same line – e.g. numeric, character, or date – they need to be converted to the same data type, using a special dBASE function.

Two more blank lines are then displayed, then another title, 'ADD A NEW TRADE CUSTOMER RECORD' is displayed, followed by two more blank lines.

The WAIT command, pauses the program, until a key is pressed. This gives the user the chance to read the screen before the rest of the program executes.

The data entry screen that you designed in the last Chapter is then used.
 APPEND BLANK adds a blank record to the end of the database,

READ allows data to be inserted into the fields.

RETURN ends the program and returns to the dot prompt.
The rest of the program is explained by the comments

### Guided activity

1.   You cannot create a program using the Assist, Control Center or the dot prompt. Instead you use the dBASE Editor – a simple word processing screen.
     *We will be using the dot prompt to enter the dBASE editor and to run programs.*

     Exit to the dot prompt.
     Whenever you enter dBASE for the first time, remember to set the drive, if necessary, using the command, SET DEFAULT TO <DRIVE LETTER>

2.   Now type MODIFY COMMAND CUSTADD1 – the first program we are going to create.
     Notes:   Remember that you can abbreviate dBASE commands to the first four letters e.g. MODI COMM.

              You can recall and re-execute commands using the up arrow key.

     *Editing Keys.*

     You will be taken into the Dbase text editing screen – the following editing keys can be used:

         Ctrl-N            insert a blank line above cursor

| | |
|---|---|
| Ctrl-Y | delete line where cursor currently placed |
| End | go to end of line |
| Esc | exit without saving |
| Ctrl-End | exit and save |

In addition, the Arrow, Backspace, Delete, Ins, and PgUp/PgDn keys may be used.

 the F10 key accesses the pull-down menus at the top of the screen.

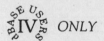

> Mouse users – you can:
>
> a.  click on the menus to open them.
>
> b.  click on the lines of a program to relocate the cursor.
>
> c.  drag the mouse to highlight the lines of a program.

Remember to leave spaces between the words of the command.
Remember always to press the Return key after every line.

3.   Type the program CUSTADD1 as shown above in the introduction.
When you have finished press Ctrl-End to exit from the file and save it to disk.
Confirm that it has been saved by typing DIR *.PRG. This will list all the
program files on disk.
Note that although it is not necessary to add the extension .PRG when you create
the file, the DIR command requires that you state the type of file you want to list
– .DBF, .PRG, .MDX etc.

4.   Now run the program using the command DO CUSTADD1.

IV *ONLY*

> The first time you run a new (or modified) program you will see a 'Compiling'
> message on the screen.
> dBASE IV takes your program and compiles it – converts it into machine code –
> the series of binary digits (0's and 1's) that the computer's processor
> understands.

If you have typed the commands successfully the two lines of the introductory
screen should appear on the screen, followed by the system prompt created by the
WAIT command,
' Press any key to continue '.

5.   Press a key and the CUSTSCRN data entry screen should appear with the fields
blank, ready for you to add a new customer record.
Now enter a new record (supply the details yourself) and the program will
automatically end and save the record.

If there is an error in the program, then accept the Cancel option and modify the
program in the way described in the Independent Activity that follows.

**Independent activity**

1.  Type the command MODI COMM CUSTADD1 to edit the program.

    Using Ctrl-N, insert extra comment lines at suitable points to explain the action of the program.

2.  Insert the command CLEAR to clear the screen before the first blank line is displayed.
    Insert another CLEAR command to clear the screen after you have finished adding the record.

3.  Save the edited program, and run it again, noting the effect of the CLEAR commands.

---

**Summary of commands used**

| | |
|---|---|
| *MODIFY COMMAND < FILE NAME >* | *Create or edit a program* |
| *DO < FILE NAME >* | *Runs a program* |
| *? < EXPRESSION >* | *Display on screen* |
| *WAIT* | *Pauses program operation until a key is pressed* |
| *DATE ()* | *Retrieves system date* |
| *DTOC ()* | *converts date to characters* |
| *\** | *indicates a comment line* |
| *APPEND BLANK* | *adds blank record to end of database* |
| *READ* | *allows on-screen data entry* |
| *CLEAR* | *clears screen* |
| *RETURN* | *ends program* |
| *Text editing commands:* | see guided activity above |

---

## Activity 2 *Programming for database maintenance*

### Objectives

1.  To create programs to edit and delete records.

2.  To position user input/output at specified screen locations

3.  To handle error messages.

4.  To copy programs.

### Introduction

In Activity 1 you created a simple program and saved it to a program file –CUSTADD1.PRG.

Activity 2: Programming for database maintenance

You then ran it and learned how to edit the commands in the program.

In this activity we will extend some of the ideas from the first program and learn how to write programs to edit and delete records in the TRADCUST database.

Study the following program CUSTED1 —

```
*
* PROGRAM CUSTED1.PRG
* < PROGRAMMER NAME AND CREATION/MODIFICATION DATE >
* PROMPTS USER FOR SURNAME AND INITIALS
* THEN CALLS SCREEN FORM CUSTSCRN
* ALLOWS USER TO EDIT EXISTING RECORD
*
SET DATE BRITISH
* CLEAR SCREEN, OPEN DATABASE,
CLEAR
USE TRADCUST
* INITIALISE MEMORY VARIABLES
STORE SPACE (15) TO MSURNAME
STORE SPACE (3) TO MINITIALS
* POSITION PROMPTS AND INPUTS ON SCREEN
@ 5,20 SAY 'INPUT CUSTOMER SURNAME' GET MSURNAME
@ 7,20 SAY 'INPUT INITIALS' GET MINITIALS
READ
* USE SCREEN FORM FOR EDITING
SET FORMAT TO CUSTSCRN
* EDIT RECORD THAT MATCHES USER INPUT
EDIT FOR MSURNAME = SURNAME .AND. MINITIALS = INITIALS
CLOSE DATABASES
CLEAR
RETURN
```

*Explanation of the Program.*

As before, comments are used to divide up and explain the various sections of the program – do this in all future programs.

The first new idea in the program is the use of memory variables.

For users to retrieve a record that they want to edit, they must first input the customer name or reference number.

The program will then try to match them against names held in the database.

Two character variables are used – MSURNAME and MINITIALS to hold user input.

A *memory variable* is merely a named part of the computer's main memory used to store data temporarily.

It is called a 'variable' for short, because any value can be assigned to it.

127

The STORE command is used to *initialise* a variable, i.e. assign it an initial value, name and type.

SPACE is used to initialise a character variable, 0 would be used for a numeric variable.

A memory variable may be up to 10 characters long, must begin with a letter, and contain no blanks.

Try to use memorable, descriptive names, not just, say, NUM1 or VAR1.

As we are using the variables to match fields in the database, it is a good convention to prefix the database field name with an M – MSURNAME, MINITIALS etc.

(You cannot use the same name for a variable as for the field)

*The dBASE Screen – SAY and GET.*

In the previous program CUSTADD1 we used the ? command to display data on the screen.

More complex displays require that user prompts and responses be placed at specified screen positions.

The @ or 'at' command is used to place information at a more precise screen location.

The dBASE screen consists of:

❐    80 vertical positions or columns, numbered from 0 to 79

❐    25 horizontal positions or rows, numbered from 0 to 24

Any screen position can be identified by these two coordinates – the row followed by the column number – e.g. @ 5,20 means 6 rows down, 21 columns across.

SAY is an output command, used to display text, variables or fields on the screen.

GET is an input command, used to tell dBASE to accept input – in this case the variables holding the surname and initials.

READ must always follow a GET command.

READ lets you actually enter or edit the information on screen.

The EDIT command then tries to match the values of the two variables, MSURNAME and MINITIALS, against values held in these fields in the TRADCUST database.

It will compare each record in the file for a match, and, if successful, will display the record using the CUSTSCRN screen form, ready for editing.

The RETURN command ends the program and returns you to the dot prompt.

**Guided activities**

1.    Type MODIFY COMMAND CUSTED1 at the dot prompt.
      Enter the program as shown above.
      Exit and save the program as in Activity 1. Now run the program using the DO command.
      If you have made any errors the program may not compile or run – see the activities that follow for more on these.

2.    Type in the surname of any customer, press Return.
      Now type the initials and press Return again.
      The record is displayed on screen ready for editing. If not:
      a. check the spelling of the name,
      b. browse the database to check its existence,

c. make sure that the cases – upper or lower – match.
Press Esc to terminate the program.

3. *ᵈᴮᴬˢᴱ ᵁˢᴱᴿˢ*IV *only. Dealing with compilation errors*

Display the program using MODI COMM CUSTED1.
Amend the command EDIT to EDI (i.e remove the final 'T')
Exit and save.
Now run the program again, and the compiler will detect the syntax error that
we have introduced, and display an error message:
' Error in line <N>. Unrecognised command Verb' and will display the incorrect
line.
Accept the cancel option offered, and return to the dot prompt.

4. *ᵈᴮᴬˢᴱ ᵁˢᴱᴿˢ*III *only. Dealing with run time errors.*

Alter the name of the Variable MSURNAME to MSURNAM.
Save and run the program again.
The program encounters an undefined variable and displays the error message
'Variable not found : MSURNAM '
Accept the Cancel option offered, and correct the error that we have introduced.

5. Most errors are of this trivial type, and can be corrected in this way.

**Independent activity**

1. Using the @ SAY command, include 2 suitable screen heading lines similar to the
ones used in the CUSTADD1 program in Activity 1.
i.e. company name and date and the purpose of the program – to edit a customer
record.

2. We will now create a program to delete a customer record by copying and
modifying the CUSTED1 program.
Issue the following command at the dot prompt:
COPY FILE CUSTED1.PRG TO CUSTDEL1.PRG
(this command can be used for all types of dBASE files, but the file extensions
must be included)

3. Using MODI COMM CUSTDEL1 make the following changes to the CUSTDEL1
program:
Change the comments and the screen titles.
Remove the SET FORMAT command – we do not want to delete the record using
the screen form.
Alter the EDIT command to DELETE.
Exit from and save the program.

4. Your program should now mark selected customer records for deletion, test this
as follows:
At the dot prompt use RECALL ALL to recall any records already marked for
deletion.

Now run CUSTDEL1 and enter the surname and initials of a customer. You should get a 'records deleted' message.
Browse the TRADCUST database and, using the status bar, confirm that the record(s) has been marked for deletion.

Now run the program again and enter the same initials and surname – this time the message is 'No records deleted' – marked records cannot be marked a second time.

5.  At the moment the record cannot be seen before the DELETE command executes. Insert a LIST command in the program to display the record(s) that will be marked for deletion.

    Hints – the command must use the same conditions as the DELETE command i.e. LIST FOR MSURNAME = SURNAME .AND. MINITIALS = INITIALS
    If you insert a WAIT command after the LIST command – see CUSTADD1 – the program will pause so that you can read the customer details.

6.  We now have our three essential database maintenance programs:-

    | | |
    |---|---|
    | CUSTADD1 | Add a customer record |
    | CUSTED1 | Edit a customer record |
    | CUSTDEL1 | Delete a customer record |

    In the next activity we will create a fourth standard program, CUSTDET1 that lists customer details, but does not permit any changes or deletions.

---

**Summary of commands used.**

*STORE < VALUE > TO < VARIABLE NAME >*
> *Stores an initial value to a memory variable.*

*@ < Row,Column > SAY < EXPRESSION >*
> *Displays information at specified row,column position on screen.*

*@ < Row,Column > GET < EXPRESSION >*
> *Allows input of data into a memory variable or data field at a specified row,column position on screen.*

*READ*  *Follows a GET command and allows entry /editing of memory variables*

*COPY FILE < ORIGINAL FILE NAME >.PRG TO < NEW FILE NAME >.PRG*
> *Copy a program file under a new name.*

*RETURN*  *Ends the program and returns control to the dot prompt or calling program.*

*EDIT FOR <CONDITIONS>*
> *Allows editing of records matching conditions.*

---

# Activity 3 *Locating and displaying records*

### Objectives

1.  To design a screen using SAY and GET commands.
2.  To convert date and numeric variables to character strings.

### Introduction

Below is program CUSTDET1.PRG, which allows customer details to be displayed but not amended.
This is useful for staff who may need to refer to customer information but who do not have the authority to change it.

```
*
* PROGRAM CUSTDET1.PRG
* <PROGRAMMER NAME AND CREATION/MODIFICATION DATE >
* PROMPTS USER FOR SURNAME AND INITIALS
* ALLOWS USER TO DISPLAY EXISTING RECORD
*
SET DATE BRITISH
* CLEAR SCREEN, OPEN DATABASE
CLEAR
USE TRADCUST
* INITIALISE MEMORY VARIABLES
STORE SPACE (15) TO MSURNAME
STORE SPACE (3) TO MINITIALS
* POSITION PROMPTS AND INPUTS ON SCREEN
@ 1,20 SAY 'QUALITY WINES      DATE:- '+DTOC(DATE())
@ 3,20 SAY 'VIEW A CUSTOMER RECORD'
@ 5,20 SAY 'INPUT CUSTOMER SURNAME' GET MSURNAME
@ 7,20 SAY 'INPUT INITIALS' GET MINITIALS
READ
* CLEAR SCREEN TO DISPLAY CUSTOMER DETAILS
@ 5,20 CLEAR
* LOCATE RECORD
LOCATE FOR MSURNAME = SURNAME .AND. MINITIALS = INITIALS
* DISPLAY THE CUSTOMER DETAILS ON SCREEN
@ 8,20 SAY 'CUSTOMER REFERENCE IS    ' + CUSTREF
@ 10,20 SAY 'CUSTOMER NAME IS    ' + INITIALS + SURNAME
```

```
            @ 12,20 SAY 'CREDIT LIMIT IS    ' + STR(CREDLIM)
            @ 14,20 SAY 'LAST ORDER IS    ' +DTOC(LASTORD)
          . @ 16,20 SAY 'EXTENDED CREDIT ?'
            @ 16,39 SAY EXCREDIT
            ?
            ?
            WAIT
            CLOSE DATABASES
            CLEAR
            RETURN
```

*Explanation of the program.*

Like the CUSTED1 program it prompts the user for the customer surname and initials, and holds them in two memory variables – MSURNAME and MINITIALS.

A new command LOCATE is then used to find the matching database record. LOCATE, if successful, moves the file pointer to the record, but does not display it.

Notice that you can use the CLEAR command with coordinates to clear part of the screen.

A number of SAY commands then display the fields on the screen – SAY can be used in a number of ways:
Compare the code above with the screen display it produces for customer J WILSON – see Figure 7.1

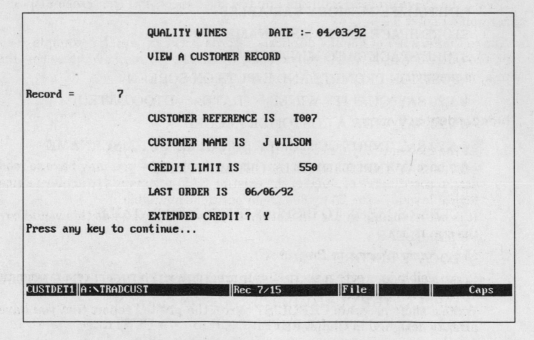

```
                  QUALITY WINES        DATE :- 04/03/92

                  VIEW A CUSTOMER RECORD


Record =       7

                  CUSTOMER REFERENCE IS    T007

                  CUSTOMER NAME IS    J WILSON

                  CREDIT LIMIT IS          550

                  LAST ORDER IS    06/06/92

                  EXTENDED CREDIT ?  Y
Press any key to continue...




CUSTDET1 A:\TRADCUST              Rec 7/15       File               Caps
```

Figure 7.1

" @ 8,20 SAY 'CUSTOMER REFERENCE IS' + CUSTREF "
This command displays the words 'CUSTOMER REFERENCE IS' on line 8, column
20, immediately followed by the customer reference field itself – CUSTREF.

" @ 10,20 SAY 'CUSTOMER NAME IS' + INITIALS + SURNAME"
This command displays two field values on screen – INITIALS and SURNAME; the +
sign serves to link them.

" @ 12,20 SAY 'CREDIT LIMIT IS' + STR(CREDLIM) "
CREDLIM is a numeric field, and before it can be displayed on the same line as the
string of text – 'CREDIT LIMIT IS' – it must be converted to text too, using the STR()
function.

" @ 14,20 SAY 'LAST ORDER IS' +DTOC(LASTORD) "
Similarly date fields, such as LASTORD, must be converted to text, using the date-to-
character function DTOC(), if they appear on the same line as a text string.

" @ 16,20 SAY 'EXTENDED CREDIT?' "

" @ 16,39 SAY EXCREDIT "

These two lines show how data type conversion can be avoided.
If you use two SAY commands for the same line (16) then you can place a logical
variable – EXCREDIT – on the same line as a text string – 'EXTENDED CREDIT? '.
However the relative positions of the two elements on the same line need careful
calculation if they are not to overlap.

### Guided activity

Create the above program and run and test it. If successful the screen display should
resemble Figure 7.1.

Notice that it will not display duplicate records – if there are, for example, 2 customers
on file called J Wilson, it will only display the first – we shall overcome this limitation
in a later activity.

### Independent activities

1.  At the moment only 6 fields of the database are displayed.
    Add more SAY commands so that all are displayed – you may have to modify the
    screen coordinates of some of the existing SAY commands to achieve a neat
    logical layout in the 25 by 80 screen positions available.
    It is not advisable to use the bottom two rows, 23 and 24 as this would cover up
    the status bar.

2.  *Using Report Forms in Programs*

    It is possible to create a short simple program which runs a report form that has
    already been created.
    Write a short program CREDLIST to run the printed report that you have
    already designed in Chapter 6.

133

You will need to clear the screen and put a message on the screen telling the user that the report is being run first.

Then use the commands:

USE TRADCUST INDEX NAMETOWN
REPORT FORM CREDREP

---

**Summary of functions and commands used**

| | |
|---|---|
| *STR()* | converts numeric data to character string |
| *DTOC()* | converts date to character string |
| *LOCATE FOR < CONDITIONS >* | finds first record matching the condition |
| *@ <ROW,COLUMN> CLEAR* | clears the screen from the stated coordinates |

---

## Activity 4 *Decisions and conditions – IF...ELSE...ENDIF*

### Objectives

1. To program for user choice using If conditions.
2. To convert lower to upper case.

### Introduction

A major limitation of our programs so far is their lack of user choice.

What, for example, if the user runs the wrong program?

He/she should be offered the choice of not going ahead with editing, adding or deleting a record.

What if the record cannot be located in the database?

A message should inform the user of this.

We need, in other words to provide decision making in the program.

The program should not only prompt the user for a response, but evaluate it, and act accordingly.

In common with other programming languages dBASE offers the IF construction, allowing the program to respond to certain conditions and take alternative routes.

The edit program CUSTED1 can be modified to include IF conditions and renamed CUSTED2.

It is shown below with full comments and the new commands in bold.

```
*
* PROGRAM CUSTED2.PRG
* < PROGRAMMER NAME AND CREATION/MODIFICATION DATE >
* PROMPTS USER FOR SURNAME AND INITIALS
* THEN CALLS SCREEN FORM CUSTSCRN
* ALLOWS USER TO EDIT EXISTING RECORD
*
SET DATE BRITISH
* CLEAR SCREEN, OPEN DATABASE,
```

```
            CLEAR
            USE TRADCUST
            * INITIALISE MEMORY VARIABLES
            STORE SPACE (15) TO MSURNAME
            STORE SPACE (3) TO MINITIALS
            STORE SPACE (1) TO CHOICE
            @ 1,20 SAY 'QUALITY WINES DATE:' + DTOC (DATE())
            @ 3,20 SAY 'EDIT A CUSTOMER RECORD'
            * OFFER USER THE CHOICE TO QUIT EDITING
            @ 5,20 SAY 'GO AHEAD? (Y/N)' GET CHOICE
            READ
            * IF USER RESPONDS 'Y' THEN CONTINUE PROGRAM
            IF UPPER(CHOICE) = 'Y'
                * POSITION PROMPTS AND INPUTS ON SCREEN
                @ 5,20 SAY 'INPUT CUSTOMER SURNAME' GET MSURNAME
                @ 7,20 SAY 'INPUT INITIALS' GET MINITIALS
                READ
                * USE SCREEN FORM FOR EDITING
                SET FORMAT TO CUSTSCRN
                EDIT FOR SURNAME = UPPER (MSURNAME) AND. UPPER(MINITIALS)=INITIALS
            * ANY OTHER RESPONSE – END IF CONDITION
            ELSE
            ENDIF
            * CLEAR SCREEN, CLOSE DATABASE, END PROGRAM
            CLEAR
            CLOSE DATABASES
            RETURN
```

*Explanation of the program*

There are 3 main steps here in setting up a condition:

a.  We initialise a variable CHOICE to hold the user's one letter response – Y or N.

b.  Then, using the SAY command, we display a 3 line screen offering the user the choice of continuing or not.

c.  The IF command evaluates the choice – if the response is 'y' or 'Y' (the UPPER function converts to upper case) the next part of the program executes.
    If the user's response is not a 'y' or a 'Y' then the program skips to the ELSE condition which deals with any other response – the user keying in an 'n', 'N' or any other letter – by ending the IF condition with an ENDIF.

The rest of the program then executes unconditionally.
The syntax of IF...ELSE...ENDIF is therefore straightforward.

135

Common pitfalls are:

a.  forgetting to end the IF with an ENDIF – indenting the commands within the IF... ENDIF command (see program) improves readability and makes your code easier to check – do this from now on.

b.  not allowing for all possibilities – ELSE should cover any other letter being input – merely testing for a Y or an N could cause the program to crash if the user, say, input an M by mistake.

## Guided activities

1.  Copy the program CUSTED1.PRG under the new name CUSTED2.PRG
    Make the above amendments shown in bold.
    It is o.k. if the EDIT command extends over two lines, but do not press Return after the first line – this creates two incomplete commands.

2.  Run the new program.
    Test that the initial choice offered responds correctly to a range of input – 'y', 'Y', 'n', 'N' or any other input.

3.  Test that the surname and initials will still locate a record if entered in lower case.

## Independent activity

Copy your program CUSTDEL1.PRG to a new program CUSTDEL2.PRG.
Modify the CUSTDEL2 program along the lines of CUSTED2 to allow the user the initial choice to end the program.

Run and test the program as above.

---

### Summary of Commands used

*UPPER (< EXPRESSION >)*

> *converts text to upper case*

*IF < CONDITION >*
  *< COMMANDS >*
*ELSE*
  *< COMMANDS >*
*ENDIF*

> *If the IF condition is true, then all commands between If and ELSE are executed.*
> *If the IF condition is false, then all the commands between ELSE and ENDIF are ignored. The program then continues with the commands after the ENDIF.*

---

# Activity 5 *More conditions – using Windows*

## Objective

1.  To use nested IF conditions.

2.  To use windows in screen displays ( $\mathcal{IV}$ only)

## Introduction

The program CUSTED2 included one IF statement.
We are going to introduce two more so that:
a. If the record does not exist the user is informed
b. When the record is retrieved the user gets a final chance to abort editing without changing the record.

Look at the following program CUSTED3.
Shown in bold are the additions to CUSTED2.

$\mathcal{IV}$ *only*. We are also going to use a window to display user messages.

A window is a predefined area of the screen that overlays the existing screen, and can be used to enter or display data. (see code in italics)

```
* PROGRAM CUSTED3.PRG
* < PROGRAMMER NAME AND CREATION/MODIFICATION DATE >
* PROMPTS USER FOR SURNAME AND INITIALS
* THEN CALLS SCREEN FORM CUSTSCRN
* DISPLAYS MESSAGE IF RECORD NOT FOUND
* GIVES CHOICE TO ABORT EDITING
* CLEAR SCREEN, OPEN DATABASE, AND INITIALISE MEMORY
* VARIABLES
SET DATE BRITISH
CLEAR
USE TRADCUST
STORE SPACE (15) TO MSURNAME
STORE SPACE (3) TO MINITIALS
STORE SPACE (1) TO CHOICE
* OFFER USER THE CHOICE TO QUIT EDITING
@ 1,20 SAY 'QUALITY WINES  DATE:' + DTOC (DATE())
@ 3,20 SAY 'EDIT A CUSTOMER RECORD'
```

137

```
                    @ 5,20 SAY 'GO AHEAD? (Y/N)' GET CHOICE
                    READ
                    * IF USER RESPONDS 'Y' THEN CONTINUE PROGRAM
                    IF UPPER(CHOICE) = 'Y'
                        CLEAR
                        * POSITION PROMPTS AND INPUTS ON SCREEN
                        @ 10,20 SAY 'INPUT CUSTOMER SURNAME' GET MSURNAME
                        @ 12,20 SAY 'INPUT INITIALS' GET MINITIALS
                        READ
                        * SEARCH FOR RECORD
                    LOCATE FOR UPPER(MSURNAME) = SURNAME .AND.
                    UPPER(MINITIALS) = INITIALS
                        * IF NOT FOUND DISPLAY MESSAGE AND END PROGRAM
                        IF .NOT. FOUND()
                            CLEAR
                            @ 10,10 SAY 'RECORD DOES NOT EXIST'
                            WAIT
                            CLEAR
                            CLOSE DATABASES
                            RETURN
                        * OTHERWISE CONFIRM RECORD FOUND
                        ELSE
                        ENDIF
                    CLEAR
                    @ 8,20 SAY 'CUSTOMER REFERENCE IS' + CUSTREF
                    @ 10,20 SAY 'SURNAME IS' + SURNAME
                    @ 12,20 SAY 'INITIALS ARE' + INITIALS
                    * DEFINE AND DISPLAY A WINDOW ON SCREEN
                    DEFINE WINDOW WIND1 FROM 15,5 TO 19,75 COLOR B/W
                    ACTIVATE WINDOW WIND1
                    * DISPLAY MESSAGE IN WINDOW
                    WAIT 'EDIT THIS RECORD? (Y/N)' TO CHOICE
                    DEACTIVATE WINDOW WIND1
                        * IF CHOICE IS Y DISPLAY SCREEN AND EDIT
                        IF UPPER(CHOICE) = 'Y'
                            SET FORMAT TO CUSTSCRN
```

```
    EDIT FOR UPPER (MSURNAME) = SURNAME .AND. UPPER (MINITIALS)=INITIALS
        ELSE
        ENDIF
    * IF USER DID NOT INITIALLY CHOOSE 'Y' THEN MAIN IF
    * CONDITION ENDS
ELSE
ENDIF
CLOSE DATABASES
CLEAR
RETURN
```

*Explanation of the program*

The first IF statement is the same as in the previous program CUSTED2 – it offers
the user the option to terminate the program or to continue.
The LOCATE command attempts to match a record to the two variables.
We can then base a second IF statement on the FOUND () function, which tests
whether the LOCATE is successful.

IF .NOT. FOUND() then a message is displayed, and the program ends – ELSE the IF
statement ends and the program continues.
Note that this second and third IF statements are enclosed or 'nested' inside the first
IF – which is still continuing.
Different depths of indentation are used to confirm this – see program.
If found, the customer name and reference are confirmed on the screen.

DBASE IV USERS *only.*

A window or area of screen named WIND1 is defined next.
The size – from top left to bottom right – is given by the usual screen coordinates.
The colour of the window is also be changed for greater effect (if you have a
monochrome screen, ignore this!).
The window is then activated or displayed, and a user prompt placed in it, using a
fuller version of the WAIT command.
The window must be deactivated after use, or it will remain active after the
program finishes.

A third user choice – to edit the record or exit – is covered by a third IF command.
Notice that the first IF condition – within which the other two are nested – is finally
ended by an ENDIF, and the program ends.

A problem of this program is that it will not locate duplicate records, e.g. if there are
two J WILSON's it will only display the first.
We will deal with this problem in later activities.

### Guided activity

Copy the program CUSTED2.PRG under the new name CUSTED3.PRG
Make the alterations shown in bold to create the program shown above. dBASE III
users should omit the code in italics.
Run the new program.
Test that the choices offered respond correctly to a full range of input.

### Independent activity

Copy your program CUSTDEL2.PRG to a new program CUSTDEL3.PRG.
Modify the CUSTDEL3 program along the lines as CUSTED3 to:

a.   allow the user the initial choice to end the program.

b.   test for the record not being found.

c.   allow user to abort before the located record is deleted

Run and test the program.

---

**Summary of commands used**

*FOUND()*          tests for success of LOCATE

*WAIT '< MESSAGE >' TO < VARIABLE NAME >*

> Displays a message on the screen, pauses the program, and
> creates a variable to hold a user response.

*dBASE USERS* **IV** only

*DEFINE WINDOW < WINDOW NAME > FROM < TOP LEFT ROW,COL > TO
< BOTTOM RIGHT ROW,COL > COLOR
< FOREGROUND INITIAL / BACKGROUND INITIAL >*

> defines a window – name, size and colour – see next activity for
> range of colours.

*ACTIVATE WINDOW < WINDOW NAME >*

> places predefined window on screen – all subsequent output
> placed in window until deactivated.

*DEACTIVATE WINDOW <WINDOW NAME >*

> deactivates/removes window from screen

---

# Activity 6 *Multiple conditions – CASE...OTHERWISE...ENDCASE*

## Objectives

1. To allow the user to choose between multiple options.
2. To use colour and boxes to enhance screen displays.
3. To call a program from another program.

## Introduction

When the program has to test for more than two or three conditions, IF and ELSE can become unwieldy.

A typical situation is an on-screen menu to maintain the Quality Wines customer database, where the user can choose several options, e.g. to add, edit, delete, or list customer records.

It is possible to program such choices using the IF command, but dBASE, in common with other modern programming languages provides a simpler CASE command.

The following program, MENU1, calls 4 programs which we have already created and offers the user the fifth option to quit.

This is much simpler than calling each program individually from the dot prompt or Assist/Control Center.

```
* PROGRAM MENU1.PRG
* < PROGRAMMER NAME AND CREATION MODIFICATION DATE >
* DISPLAYS USER MENU FOR THE TRADCUST DATABASE
*
* CLEAR SCREEN, SET COLOUR, AND OPEN DATABASE
CLEAR
SET COLOR TO R/W
USE TRADCUST
* INITIALISE VARIABLE FOR USER MENU OPTION
STORE 0 TO OPTION
* DISPLAY SCREEN HEADINGS AND MENU CHOICES
@ 3,20 SAY 'QUALITY WINES DATE:' + DTOC (DATE())
@ 6,20 SAY 'TRADE CUSTOMER DATABASE – MAIN MENU'
* SET THE SCREEN COLOUR AND DRAW BOX
SET COLOR TO B/W
@ 8,5 TO 18,67
@ 10,10 SAY '1.    ADD A RECORD'
```

```
@ 10,40 SAY '2.    EDIT A RECORD'
@ 13,10 SAY '3.    VIEW A RECORD'
@ 13,40 SAY '4.    DELETE A RECORD'
@ 16,30 SAY '5.    EXIT'
@ 20,25 SAY 'ENTER AN OPTION 1 – 5'
* OPTION MUST BE A DIGIT RANGE 1 – 5
@ 20,50 GET OPTION RANGE 1,5
READ
* RESTORE COLOR TO DEFAULT
SET COLOR TO
** START THE CASE STATEMENT
DO CASE
    CASE OPTION = 1
        DO CUSTADD1
    CASE OPTION = 2
        DO CUSTED3
    CASE OPTION = 3
        DO CUSTDET1
    CASE OPTION = 4
        DO CUSTDEL3
OTHERWISE
** END CASE STATEMENT
ENDCASE
** END THE PROGRAM
CLOSE DATABASES
CLEAR
RETURN
```

*Explanation of the program*

Within the DO CASE.... END CASE statement the program tests each CASE until it finds one that is true.

For the variable OPTION it means in effect: 'If it is the case that OPTION = 1, do program CUSTADD1, if it is the case that OPTION = 2, do program CUSTED3 etc. otherwise end the case statement.'

Notice the indentation to improve readability.

Every DO CASE statement requires an ENDCASE to terminate it.

OTHERWISE is the equivalent of the ELSE in an IF statement, and should be included to trap any other possibility – in this case the user not entering a number between 1 – 5.

As an additional check, the GET command for entry of the user choice is checked using RANGE (between 1 and 5)

You may recall this from when we were designing screen forms – in previous chapters.

Notice also that GET can be given its own screen coordinates, if desired.

The DO command is used within the program to call the other programs.

Further refinements are the ability to vary the colour, and to divide up the screen by using a box. This is useful to distinguish, e.g. headings from the rest of the screen, or prompts from user input fields, but should not be overdone.

Remember to reset the colour to the default before the program ends, otherwise you will have to reset it at the dot prompt.

The colour options are listed in the Summary of Commands.

## Guided activity

Key in and run the above program MENU1.PRG.

Test that all the options work.

*Notes:*

☐   If you are using a monochrome monitor then omit the colour commands.

☐   To reset the dot prompt to its default colour, type SET COLOR TO

## Independent activitles

1.   Create a program ADDTRAN1 to add records to the TRADTRAN database – see previous Chapter 6.
Base the program on your program CUSTADD1 – use the data entry screen TRANSCRN that you created.

2.   Add a sixth user option to the MENU1 program, so that the user can call the program ADDTRAN1.

3.   ᴮᴬˢᴱ ᵁˢᴱᴿˢ IV *only*

You may wish to improve the screen display further by using windows – see previous activity.

4.   You may have noticed that a 0 – the initial value of the OPTION variable – is displayed on the main menu screen.
Suppress this by using the command SET TALK OFF at the start of the program.
SET TALK ON again at the end of the program.

## Summary of Commands Used

*SET COLOR ON/OFF*        Sets colour on or off.

*SET COLOR TO < FOREGROUND COLOUR INITIAL >*

Sets screen characters to specified colour on a neutral background.

*SET COLOR TO < FOREGROUND COLOUR INITIAL /*

*BACKGROUND COLOUR INITIAL >*

Selects foreground and background colours.

*SET COLOR TO*

Restores colour to default.

*@ < ROW,COLUMN > TO < ROW,COLUMN>*

Draws a box on screen from top left to bottom right coordinate.

*SET TALK ON/OFF*

Does/does not display the content of memory variables on screen.

Colour options:

> *B = Blue,     G = Green,     BG = Cyan,*
> *R = Red,     BR = Magenta,     GR = Yellow,*
> *W = White,     * = Flashing     + = Bold*

Monochrome Options:

> *W+ = Bold,     /W = Reverse,     W* = Blinking*

*DO CASE*

   *CASE < CONDITION >*

     *< COMMANDS >*

   *CASE < CONDITION >*

     *< COMMANDS > etc..*

*[OTHERWISE]*

     *<COMMANDS>*

*ENDCASE*

Evaluates a number of choices for their truth. If none of the CASE statements are true then commands following the optional OTHERWISE are executed.
Then ENDCASE terminates CASE command and continues with program.

# Chapter 8

# More advanced programming in dBASE

**Introduction to the chapter**

*This final Chapter adds some further programming skills.*
*You will learn:*

    a.  *to make a program execute more than once,*

    b.  *to use one database to update another,*

    c.  *methods of improving the screen display.*

    d.  *a simple password security program.*

*The Chapter ends with some final exercises consolidating the skills that you have gained.*

## Activity 1 *Looping or iteration – DO WHILE...ENDDO*

### Objectives

1.     To use a DO loop to run a program more than once.
2.     To set the system defaults.

### Introduction

All our programs so far have had a major limitation – they are a simple sequence of commands that are executed once and then terminate.

To process another record – view, edit, delete etc. – the program must be run again.

In the case of the main menu program MENU1, the user may well want to, say, choose the edit option, then return to the main menu and call another option, e.g. delete.

At the moment the program terminates after one option has been selected.

So we need a means to keep repeating a program rather than ending after executing once.

Such a process is called looping or iteration, and is built into all major programming languages.

The dBASE command is:

DO WHILE – do while a condition remains true –

ENDDO – repeat the loop if the condition is still true.

This is easy to build into the main menu program as follows:

```
* PROGRAM MENU2.PRG
* < PROGRAMMER NAME AND CREATION / MODIFICATION DATE >
* DISPLAYS USER MENU FOR THE TRADCUST DATABASE
* USES DO LOOP TO REPEAT
*
* SET SYSTEM DEFAULTS
* SET STATUS OFF
* SET SCOREBOARD OFF
* SET ESCAPE OFF
*
* CLEAR SCREEN, SET COLOUR, AND OPEN DATABASE
CLEAR
SET COLOR TO R/W
USE TRADCUST
SET TALK OFF
* INITIALISE VARIABLE FOR USER MENU CHOICE
STORE 0 TO OPTION
*
* REPEAT UNTIL USER INPUTS OPTION 5
DO WHILE OPTION <> 5
    * DISPLAY SCREEN HEADINGS AND MENU CHOICES
    @ 3,20 SAY 'QUALITY WINES DATE:' + DTOC (DATE())
    @ 6,20 SAY 'TRADE CUSTOMER DATABASE – MAIN MENU'
    * SET COLOR AND DRAW BOX
    SET COLOR TO G/W
    @ 8,5 TO 18,67 COLOR G/W
    @ 10,10 SAY '1. ADD A RECORD'
    @ 10,40 SAY '2. EDIT A RECORD'
    @ 13,10 SAY '3. VIEW A RECORD'
    @ 13,40 SAY '4. DELETE A RECORD'
    @ 16,30 SAY '5. EXIT'
    @ 20,25 SAY 'ENTER AN OPTION 1 – 5'
    * OPTION MUST BE A DIGIT RANGE 1 – 5
    @ 20,50 GET OPTION RANGE 1,5 PICTURE '9'
    READ
    * RESTORE COLOR TO DEFAULT
```

```
        SET COLOR TO W/B
        ** START THE CASE STATEMENT
        DO CASE
            CASE OPTION = 1
                DO CUSTADD1
            CASE OPTION = 2
                DO CUSTED3
            CASE OPTION = 3
                DO CUSTDET1
            CASE OPTION = 4
                DO CUSTDEL3
            OTHERWISE
            ** END CASE STATEMENT
        ENDCASE
    ** END LOOP WHEN A 5 IS INPUT
    ENDDO
    * RESTORE SYSTEM DEFAULTS
    SET TALK ON
    SET STATUS ON
    SET SCOREBOARD ON
    SET ESCAPE ON
    ** END THE PROGRAM
    CLOSE DATABASES
    CLEAR
    RETURN
```

*Explanation of program*

This program MENU2 adds a DO WHILE loop to MENU1.

The command is: DO WHILE OPTION <> 5

i.e. keep doing the program while the value for the variable OPTION is not 5.

As the variable OPTION is initially set to 0, the commands within the DO loop will execute at least once.

When the end of the loop is reached – ENDDO, the value of OPTION is tested again.

If the condition is still true, i.e. OPTION still does not equal 5, the DO loop 'ends' in the sense that it goes back to the beginning and starts again – iterates.

If the condition is now false and the user has entered 5, (i.e. OPTION = 5) the DO loop 'ends' in the literal sense – it will stop repeating and move on to the rest of the program.

Notice that the commands inside the DO loop are indented to improve readability.

### Guided activity

Copy MENU1.PRG and rename it MENU2.PRG.
Modify it as shown above – the new commands and comments are shown in bold.
Run the program and test that the called programs return you to the main menu.

When you are sure that the program does not crash, remove the asterisk or star symbol from the three lines:
SET STATUS OFF, SET SCOREBOARD OFF, and SET ESCAPE OFF
This changes them from comment lines to executable commands.
If you run the program again you will see that the status bar – which the user does not need to see – is set off.

SET ESCAPE OFF prevents the user from aborting the program prematurely by pressing the Escape key – a good precaution as it prevents files being left open or defaults such as colour from being unrestored.
As with other defaults, they should be restored before the program ends, and not used until the program has been properly tested.

### Independent activities

1. You have now produced a main menu which loops or iterates until the user enters the value 5 for the variable OPTION.
   Another form of iteration involves setting up an 'endless' loop using DO WHILE .T. and ENDDO.
   This means literally 'do while the logical variable .T. is true'.
   As this is true by definition, the loop continues indefinitely – there is no built in condition to end it.
   We therefore need the command EXIT to exit from the loop.
   The following program CUSTADD2 adds such a loop to the program CUSTADD1

2. Copy the program CUSTADD1.PRG, renaming it CUSTADD2.PRG.
   Then make the modifications shown in bold.
   Run and test the program.

```
* PROGRAM CUSTADD2.PRG

* < PROGRAMMER NAME AND CREATION MODIFICATION DATE >

* CALLS TITLE SCREEN THEN SCREEN FORM CUSTSCRN

* ALLOWS USER TO APPEND NEW RECORD

*

* SET UP ENDLESS LOOP
DO WHILE .T.
     CLEAR
     ?
     ?
```

```
* DISPLAY COMPANY NAME AND CURRENT DATE
? 'QUALITY WINES DATE: '+DTOC(DATE())
?
?
? 'ADD A NEW TRADE CUSTOMER RECORD '
?
?
WAIT
* OPEN DATABASE AND SCREEN ENTRY FORM
USE TRADCUST
SET FORMAT TO CUSTSCRN
* ADD BLANK RECORD
APPEND BLANK
READ
WAIT 'ADD ANOTHER RECORD? (Y/N)' TO CHOICE
    IF UPPER(CHOICE) = 'Y'
        LOOP
    ELSE
        EXIT
ENDIF
* END OF DO WHILE .T. LOOP
ENDDO
*

CLOSE DATABASES
CLEAR
RETURN
```

*Explanation of the program*

EXIT and LOOP can be used to either end or repeat a do loop.
The EXIT command exits from a DO loop to the first command after the ENDDO
EXIT is usually executed conditionally from an IF command.
In this case, if the user keys in any other character except a 'Y' then the EXIT
command terminates the DO loop, and continues with the last three commands in
the program.
If the user keys a 'Y' then the LOOP command jumps back to the start of the DO
loop.
Although LOOP and EXIT can be used with any type of DO loop, they should be
used with caution – used too often and one ends up with a program that is always
jumping in and out of loops and is difficult to read and maintain.

It is usually possible to build the conditions that will continue or end the loop into the DO WHILE statement itself. The program MENU2 above is an example of this.

A good general rule is that a DO loop should have only one entry and exit point – if you are having to make excessive use of EXIT and LOOP then you probably need to re-think your program design.

3.  Modify the program MENU2.PRG so that it calls the new program CUSTADD2.PRG instead of CUSTADD1.

---

**Summary of Commands Used**

*DO WHILE < CONDITIONS > ENDDO*

> *Defines a section of program to be repeated, and under what conditions.*

*LOOP*      *starts the DO loop again*

*EXIT*      *exits the DO loop, to first command after ENDDO*

*SET STATUS OFF*

> *sets off the status line at the bottom of the screen during program execution.*

*SET SCOREBOARD OFF*

> *used with SET STATUS OFF to suppress keyboard settings eg Caps, Ins, being displayed on screen*

*SET ESCAPE OFF*

> *de-activates the Escape key during program execution*

---

 Go to Activity 3.

 *Only* Carry on with Activity 2.

# Activity 2 *Using multiple databases 1. Updating (IV)*

### Objective

To update a database using data held in another.

### Introduction

All the dBASE operations that you have learnt so far, including programming, have used a single database.

There are, however, many situations where working with multiple databases is important. A typical one would be the updating of a master file by a transaction file. The TRADCUST database is a case in point. It holds important information about Quality Wines' trade customers – name, address, credit rating etc.

Most of these fields can be regarded as *standing information* – the information held will not change very frequently.

An exception is the BALS field that holds the customer's balance – how much he owes the company. This will change every time he receives more goods on credit or settles a bill.

Rather than alter this field directly, the day to day transactions are held in the database TRADTRAN – see Chapter 6, Activity 2.

Then, at suitable intervals, the batch of transactions held in the transaction file are used to update the master file. This type of processing is known as batch processing. We will use an update query or view to do this.

## Guided activity

1.  First we will create the View, then write a program to run it.
    At the dot prompt issue the command, CREATE VIEW UPDATBAL
    You are taken into the View design screen – to recap on this see Chapter 3, Activity 4.

2.  Use the F10 key or mouse to open the Layout menu if necessary.
    Select the option 'Add file to query'. Select the TRADTRAN database first.
    Repeat these steps to select the TRADCUST database.
    You should now have two file skeletons at the top of the query design screen – see Figure 8.1.

3.  Next we must link the two databases on their common field.

    Move the cursor to the CUSTREF field in the TRADTRAN file skeleton and press Return.
    Open the Layout menu again, this time choose the option, 'Create link by pointing'. The word 'Link1' appears in the CUSTREF field of the TRADTRAN file skeleton.

    Now, using F4 and Tab keys or mouse, move the cursor to the CUSTREF field in the *TRADCUST* database, and press Return.
    'Link1' now appears in both CUSTREF fields – the databases have been linked on their common field

4.  The final step is to specify the update we want to perform.
    Open the Update menu. Select the option 'Specify update operation'
    A further menu appears, select the option, 'Replace values in Tradcust.dbf'.
    The word 'Replace' appears in the TRADCUST file skeleton.

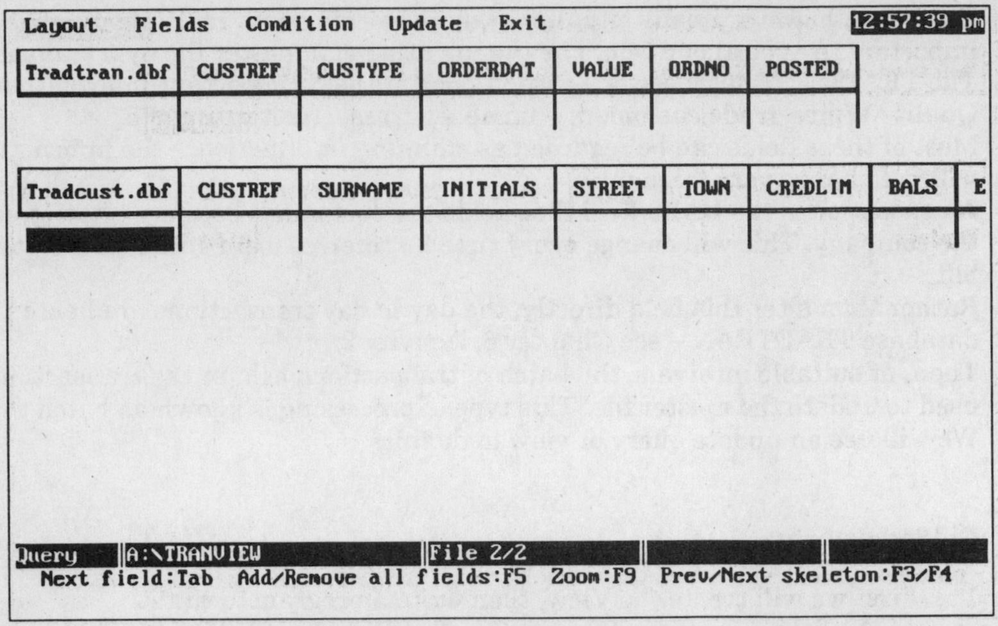

Figure 8.1

5. Move the cursor to the BALS field in the TRADCUST file skeleton (it may not currently be visible).
   We want to add the contents of the VALUE field in the TRADTRAN database, which holds the value of an order, to the customer's current balance in the TRADCUST database.
   Enter the replace condition: WITH BALS+VALUE

6. The other condition is that the order has not already been used to update the customer balance i.e. has not already been 'posted'.
   Move to the TRADTRAN file skeleton and enter the condition .N. in the logical field POSTED.

7. Check that your Query design screen is the same as Figure 8.2.
   Then exit and save the Query.

8. Before you run the query, open and browse each database in turn.
   Make sure that some of the POSTED fields in the TRADTRAN database have the value .F. or .N.
   Note which records are going to be updated and the changes in value expected.
   Use the SUM command to find the pre-update values for the BALS and the VALUE fields in the two databases. (Note: SET TALK ON must be operative for the sum to be displayed)

9. Now run the query with the command, DO UPDATBAL.UPD
   After you have run the query, examine the post- update values for the BALS fields.
   Have the balances been successfully updated?
   Sum the BALS field again.
   Does the difference in the total after the update equal the sum of VALUE fields?
   i.e. does new BALS total – old BALS total = sum of VALUE fields for unposted records?

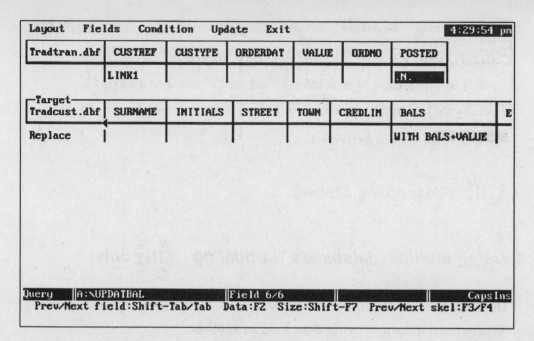

| Layout | Fields | Condition | Update | Exit | | 4:29:54 pm |
|---|---|---|---|---|---|---|

| Tradtran.dbf | CUSTREF | CUSTYPE | ORDERDAT | VALUE | ORDNO | POSTED |
|---|---|---|---|---|---|---|
| | LINK1 | | | | | .N. |

| Target Tradcust.dbf | SURNAME | INITIALS | STREET | TOWN | CREDLIM | BALS | E |
|---|---|---|---|---|---|---|---|
| Replace | | | | | | WITH BALS+VALUE | |

| Query | A:\UPDATBAL | | Field 6/6 | | | | Caps Ins |
|---|---|---|---|---|---|---|---|

Prev/Next field:Shift-Tab/Tab   Data:F2   Size:Shift-F7   Prev/Next skel:F3/F4

Figure 8.2

**Independent activities**

The office staff at Quality Wines would not wish to run the update query from the dot prompt.
Write a short program, CUSBAL1 incorporating the following:

1. Suitable screen titles.

2. A prompt giving the user the opportunity to cancel the update before the update query is run.

3. A message to the user 'Updating Customer Balances – Please Wait'.

4. A command to run the Query.

5. It is possible to build the SUM command checks (see above) into the program so the user can check the changes.
   Do this, displaying the results of the validation on screen.

   *Hints:*

   a. To store the pre and post-update values, use the command,

      SUM < FIELDNAME > to < VARIABLE NAME >

   b. Use SET TALK OFF to suppress the details of records updated being displayed on screen.

      SET TALK ON at the end of the program.

6. Clear the screen and close databases.

---

**Summary of commands used**

*SUM < FIELDNAME > to < VARIABLE NAME >*
*Adds up the values of a database field and stores it to a variable.*

---

 Now go to Activity 4.

 Go to Activity 3 below

# Activity 3 *Using multiple databases 1. Updating ( III only)*

### Objective
To update a database using data held in another.

### Introduction
All the dBASE operations that you have learnt so far, including programming, have used a single database.

There are, however, many situations where working with multiple databases is important. A typical one would be the updating of a master file by a transaction file. The TRADCUST database is a case in point. It holds important information about Quality Wines' trade customers – name, address, credit rating etc.

Most of these fields can be regarded as *standing information* – the information held will not change very frequently.

An exception is the BALS field that holds the customer's balance – how much he owes the company. This will change every time he receives more goods on credit or settles a bill.

Rather than alter this field directly, the day to day transactions are held in the database TRADTRAN – see Chapter 6, Activity 2.

Then, at suitable intervals, the batch of transactions held in the transaction file are used to update the master file. This type of processing is known as batch processing. We will use an update query or view to do this.

 **Guided activity**

You should already have a number of records in the TRADTRAN database.
Create the following update program but do not run it yet.
Note: The arrow symbol in the UPDATE command is formed from a dash – and a > symbol (no space between)

```
** PROGRAM CUSBAL1.PRG
* < PROGRAMMER NAME AND CREATION/MODIFICATION DATE >
* UPDATES MASTER FILE TRADCUST
* FROM TRANSACTION FILE TRADTRAN
* SET SYSTEM DEFAULTS
* SET SAFETY OFF
SET ESCAPE OFF
CLEAR
* OPEN TRADTRAN FIRST AND INDEX
SELECT 2
USE TRADTRAN INDEX REFDEX
* OPEN TRADCUST AND INDEX NEXT
SELECT 1
USE TRADCUST INDEX CUSTREF
* UPDATE THE CUSTOMER BALANCE IN TRADCUST
* FROM THE VALUE FIELD IN TRADTRAN
*
UPDATE ON CUSTREF FROM TRADTRAN REPLACE BALS WITH BALS +
TRADTRAN->VALUE
CLOSE DATABASES
SET SAFETY ON
SET ESCAPE ON
RETURN
```

*Explanation of the program*

dBASE III + allows you to have up to ten databases open at once, provided each one is allocated its own work area.

The SELECT command opens a work area, which can be given a reference number or letter – the last work area to be selected contains the active database.

The UPDATE command requires that the database that is being updated be the active one, hence TRADCUST is opened second, and becomes the one currently in use.

The UPDATE command also requires that the database to be updated be indexed on the key field – for TRADCUST this is CUSTREF – the field that it shares in common with the transaction file TRADTRAN.

It is not essential but desirable that the transaction file be also indexed on the same key field; updating is quicker when both databases are in the same indexed sequence.

The UPDATE command is fairly long and complex; it is best regarded as in two parts:

'UPDATE ON CUSTREF FROM TRADTRAN' identifies the databases and their key fields, it means 'update the active database (TRADCUST) using its key field (CUSTREF) from the second database (TRADTRAN)'

'REPLACE BALS WITH BALS + TRADTRAN->VALUE' identifies the updating and updated fields, it means 'replace the present value of the balance field (BALS) with the present value plus the value of the VALUE field from the TRADTRAN database.'

155

SET SAFETY OFF stops the system displaying a user prompt when the index files are about to be updated and overwritten.
It should be set on again at the end of the program.

### Independent activity

1.  Before you run the program, open and browse each database in turn.
    Note which records are going to be updated and the changes in value expected.
    Use the SUM command to find the pre-update values for the BALS and the VALUE fields in the two databases. (Note: SET TALK ON must be operative for the sum to be displayed)
    Close all databases.

2.  Now run the program .
    After you have run it, examine the post- update values for the BALS fields.
    Have the balances been successfully updated?
    Sum the BALS field again.
    Does the difference in the total after the update equal the sum of VALUE fields?
    i.e. does new BALS total – old BALS total = sum of VALUE fields for unposted records?

3.  It is possible to build the SUM command checks (see above) into the program so the user can check the changes.
    Do this, displaying the results of the validation on screen.

    Hint: To store the pre and post-update values, use the command,

    SUM < FIELDNAME > to < VARIABLE NAME >

4.  When the update has taken place, all the POSTED fields in TRADTRAN need resetting to .T.
    Do this by opening TRADTRAN again at the end of the program and using the REPLACE all command – see Chapter 6, Activity 3.

---

**Summary of commands used**

*SELECT < REFERENCE >*    *Opens and activates a work area*
*SET SAFETY ON / OFF*

> *Does / does not inform the user when a file is about to be overwritten.*

*SUM < FIELDNAME > to < VARIABLE NAME >*

> *Adds up the values of a database field and stores it to a variable.*

*UPDATE ON < KEY FIELD > FROM < UPDATING FILE > REPLACE*
*< UPDATED FIELD NAME > WITH < UPDATING FILE NAME > –>*
*< UPDATING FIELD NAME >*

> *Performs batch update on one database from another, if the transaction file is not indexed the qualifier RANDOM may be added to the end of the command.*

---

# Activity 4 *Using multiple databases 2. Advancing the screen position*

### Objectives

1. To locate duplicate records
2. To reset the row number
3. To direct program output to a printer

### Introduction

In the previous activity we used the relational power of dBASE to combine fields from two databases. We will take this a stage further in this activity.

Before a sales clerk at Quality Wines accepts a new order from a customer he/she will need to check the customer's present balance and make sure that the customer has not exceeded (or is about to exceed) their credit limit.

So the sales clerk needs to see on the screen:

1. The BALS and CREDLIM fields from the TRADCUST database.
2. The value of any orders not yet added to the customer balance – from the TRADTRAN database.

The final screen will look like Figure 8.4.

We will first create another view, then create the following program to display it – ACDISP1.PRG.

```
* PROGRAM ACDISP1.PRG
* * < PROGRAMMER NAME AND CREATION/MODIFICATION DATE >
* USES QUERY CUSTAC TO DISPLAY CUSTOMER CREDIT
* AND OUTSTANDING ORDERS
CLEAR
* SET SYSTEM DEFAULTS
SET TALK OFF
SET STATUS OFF
SET SCOREBOARD OFF
SET SAFETY OFF
SET ESCAPE OFF
SET DATE BRITISH
* INITIALISE VARIABLES
STORE SPACE (15) TO MSURNAME
STORE SPACE (4) TO MCUSTREF
STORE 0 TO UNPOSTED
STORE 0 TO TOTAL
* DISPLAY SCREEN TITLES
```

```
@ 1,15 SAY 'QUALITY WINES LTD. DATE:' +DTOC(DATE())
@ 3,15 SAY 'VIEW A TRADE CUSTOMER ACCOUNT '
?
?
* GIVE USER A CHANCE TO EXIT
WAIT 'GO AHEAD? (Y/N)' TO CHOICE
IF UPPER(CHOICE) = 'N'
    CLEAR
    RETURN
    SET COLOR TO
    SET SCOREBOARD ON
    SET SAFETY ON
    SET STATUS ON
    SET ESCAPE ON
    SET TALK ON
ELSE
ENDIF
* CLEAR SCREEN EXCEPT FOR TITLES
@ 4,1 CLEAR
* PROMPT FOR CUSTOMER REFERENCE AND SURNAME
@ 5,14 SAY 'INPUT CUSTOMER REFERENCE'
@ 5,45 GET MCUSTREF PICTURE '@! A999'
@ 7,14 SAY 'INPUT CUSTOMER SURNAME'
@ 7,45 GET MSURNAME PICTURE '@! XXXXXXXXXXXXXX'
READ
* USE VIEW OF TRADCUST/TRADTRAN DATABASES
SET VIEW TO CUSTAC
* SEARCH FOR MATCHING RECORD
LOCATE FOR MSURNAME = TRADCUST->SURNAME .AND. MCUSTREF =
CUSTREF
* RESET COLOUR
SET COLOR TO +G
* DISPLAY CUSTOMER DETAILS
@ 9,2 SAY 'CUSTOMER:  ' + INITIALS+SURNAME
@ 9,30 SAY 'ADDRESS:  ' + TRIM(STREET)
@ 9,60 SAY TOWN
```

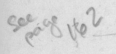

see page 162

```
@ 11,2 SAY 'CREDIT LIMIT'
@ 11,30 SAY CREDLIM
@ 13,2 SAY 'CURRENT BALANCE:'
@ 13,30 SAY BALS
* STORE BALANCE IN VARIABLE
STORE BALS TO MBALS
@ 15,2 SAY 'PLUS UNPOSTED ORDERS'
SET COLOR TO R/W
@ 15,32 SAY 'ORDER DATE'
@ 15,45 SAY 'ORDER NO.'
@ 15,58 SAY 'VALUE'
@ 15,70 SAY 'POSTED?'
* STORE ROW NUMBER IN A VARIABLE
R=17
* DISPLAY FIRST TRANSACTION RECORD FOUND
DO WHILE CUSTREF = UPPER(MCUSTREF) .AND. .NOT. POSTED
@ R,32 SAY ORDERDAT
@ R,45 SAY ORDNO
@ R,58 SAY VALUE
@ R,73 SAY POSTED
* LOOK FOR NEXT TRANSACTION RECORD
CONTINUE
* MOVE TO THE NEXT ROW ON SCREEN
R=R+1
ENDDO
* ADD UP VALUE OF ALL UNPOSTED TRANSACTIONS
SUM VALUE TO UNPOSTED FOR CUSTREF=MCUSTREF .AND. .NOT.
POSTED
* ADD TO CURRENT BALANCE TO GIVE TOTAL OWED
STORE MBALS + UNPOSTED TO TOTAL
@ R+1,24 SAY 'TOTAL DEBT OUTSTANDING'
@ R+1,46 SAY TOTAL
* GET USER TO CHECK CREDIT STATUS
@ 22,20 SAY 'CHECK CUSTOMER HAS NOT EXCEEDED CREDIT LIMIT'
WAIT
*RESET DEFAULTS AND END PROGRAM
```

```
CLEAR
CLOSE DATABASES
SET COLOR TO
SET SCOREBOARD ON
SET SAFETY ON
SET STATUS ON
SET ESCAPE ON
SET TALK ON
RETURN
```

*Explanation of Program*

This program is the longest we have created so far, and uses several new ideas:

1.  Format checks on input data.
    The customer's reference number and surname, must be entered using the correct format – otherwise the correct customer record will not be located.
    The reference code CUSTREF must consist of one capital letter, followed by 3 digits, and the surname entered in upper case.

    The A symbol represents a letter, and 9 any digit.
    X represents any character including a blank.
    The @! symbols convert letters entered in lower to upper case.

    You will remember that these templates can be used in designing screen formats, and a full list of symbols follows these activities.

    See Chapter 2, Activity 3 ( III )

    See Chapter 5, Activity 4 ( IV )

2.  Removing unwanted blanks from fields.
    To display the customer's name and address on one line, we need to remove or 'trim' any unused spaces from the right of the STREET field – otherwise the full length of the field will be displayed – 25 characters.
    The TRIM function does just this (LTRIM can be used to remove leading blanks from a field).

3.  Advancing the screen coordinates a row (or line) at a time.
    Study the screen display in Figure 8.4.
    All transaction records for customer B SMITH have been displayed at the bottom of the screen.
    To do this the program needs to print the first transaction, then move a row down the screen and print the next, and so on.
    This can be done quite simply by:

    a.  Storing the first usable row number as a variable R.

    b.  Using LOCATE to find the first transaction for B SMITH

c.  Using the SAY command to display the transaction details on this row.

d.  Locating duplicate records.
    CONTINUE is used after LOCATE to move the file pointer to the next matching record (if any).
    If there is another matching record then this must be printed on the next row.
    The loop DO WHILE CUSTREF = (UPPER)MCUSTREF ensures that this continues while matching records are found.

e.  Increasing the row number by 1 for every repetition of the loop, ensuring that on the next pass through the loop the next record printed is on a new row.
    The DO WHILE loop will end when there are no more matching records found.

**Guided activity**

$\underset{\text{\tiny BASE USERS}}{\text{III}}$ *only* – $\underset{\text{\tiny BASE USERS}}{\text{IV}}$ *go to step 7.*

1.  Using the techniques learnt in Chapter 2, Activity 4, we are going to create a new view – CUSTAC.

2.  First we need to ensure that both databases have an index on their common field – CUSTREF
    Open the database TRADTRAN.
    Then type the command: SET INDEX TO?
    Check that the index REFDEX still exists.
    Then open TRADCUST and check that the index CUSTREF still exists.
    If not create them using the command INDEX ON CUSTREF TO <NAME>.

3.  Issue the command CREATE VIEW CUSTAC and you are taken into the special Query Design Screen – see Chapter 2, Activity 4.
    A list of databases appears under the Set Up menu.
    Select TRADTRAN first as the main or 'parent' database.
    A list of index files appears next, select REFDEX. Now press the left arrow key and select the child database TRADCUST, and its index CUSTREF.

4.  Now press the right arrow key to move to the Relate menu – the parent and child databases are shown.
    Press Return to select TRADTRAN first.
    The name of the child database – TRADCUST – appears next to it.
    The prompt 'Relation Chain' appears at the bottom of the screen.
    Press Return again.
    Type the field name CUSTREF – the name of the common field.
    Press Return.

    The prompt at the bottom of the screen now reads
    ' TRADTRAN.DBF->TRADCUST.DBF'
    This is the correct parent-child relationship – see Figure 8.3.

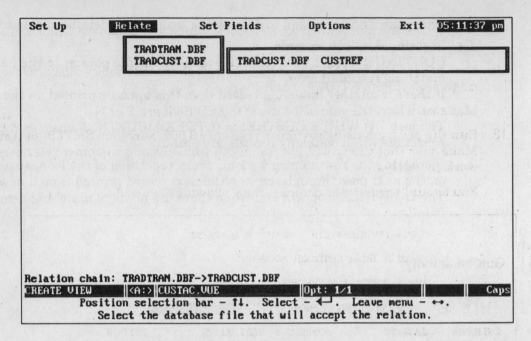

Figure 8.3

If you have made a mistake, then pressing the Esc key will take you back a step at a time.

5.    Now use the right arrow key to move to the third menu option - Set Fields.
Press Return and the fields of the TRADTRAN database are displayed.
At present all the fields are marked with an arrowhead for inclusion in the view.
Move to the CUSTYPE field, and press Return to deselect it.
Now press the right arrow key, then select the child database TRADCUST.
Select the following fields for inclusion: SURNAME, INITIALS, STREET, TOWN, CREDLIM, BALS.
Deselect the others.

6.    Finally move to the Exit option to exit and save the view.

dBASE IV USERS *Only* – (dBASE III USERS *Go to Step 11*)

7.    Using the techniques learnt in Activity 2, create a new view - CUSTAC.
First add the TRADTRAN database to the view then the TRADCUST database.

8.    Link the two databases on the CUSTREF field.

9.    From TRADTRAN include the fields, CUSTREF, ORDERDAT, ORDNO, VALUE, POSTED
From the TRADCUST database, include the fields, SURNAME, INITIALS, STREET, TOWN, CREDLIM, BALS.

10.   Exit and save this view as CUSTAC.

11. Now create the above program ACDISP1 which will use these fields to display details of the customer account.

12. Now browse the TRADTRAN database and check that the two records for customer reference T002 are still there.

    Make sure that the values for the POSTED field are F or N.

13. Run the program using customer reference T002, surname SMITH as test data. Make sure that the format checks on the surname and customer reference fields work correctly.

    You should produce the screen output shown in figure 8.4

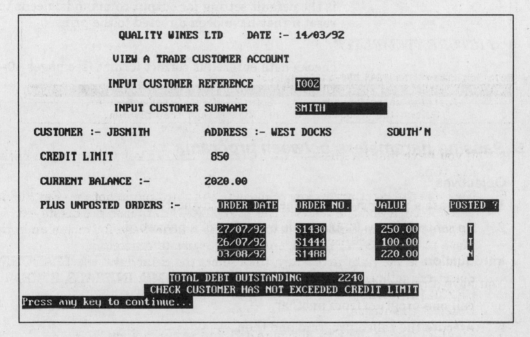

Figure 8.4

## Independent exercises

1. If the program cannot find the requested customer record, trap this using the IF .NOT. FOUND() command used in Chapter 7, Activity 5.
   Display an error message and give the user the option to exit or try again.

2. Similarly at the end of the program give the user the chance to exit or display another customer's account details.

3. If you have a printer, you can direct output to it.
   Insert the command, SET DEVICE TO PRINTER after the user has input the customer details.
   At the end of the program, include the command, SET DEVICE TO SCREEN to reset the output to your screen.

---

**Summary of commands and functions used**

| | |
|---|---|
| *TRIM() or RTRIM()* | remove trailing spaces from a character string |
| *LTRIM()* | removes leading spaces from a character string |
| *CONTINUE* | used with the LOCATE command to find any further records matching the locate condition |
| *SET DEVICE TO PRINTER* | sends subsequent output commands to the printer |
| *SET DEVICE TO SCREEN* | is the default setting for output commands; needs to be reset if they have been directed to the printer |
| *PICTURE '(TEMPLATE)'* | checks data entered is correct format (see pages 40–41 and 97 for list) |

---

## Activity 5 *Passing parameters between programs*

**Objectives**

1. To pass a parameter from one program to another.
2. To control access to programs by means of a password.

**Introduction**

You have already found that it is fairly simple to –

a. call one program from another,

b. execute the called program and then,

c. return to the calling program e.g. a main menu.

Sometimes it is useful to go one step further and pass information between programs.

This information is usually a value or range of values, such as a variable, that the user can alter, and which affects the running of the program in some way.
This is known as passing parameters.
Now that we have a menu of user options – see Activity 1 – we may want to control user access by means of a password. Thus anyone at Quality Wines may view a Customer record, but only certain people may add, delete or amend records.
Simple password security may be enough to deter casual or inexperienced users from tampering with records.
We can build password control into each separate program by passing the password to a special security program to be validated.

**Guided activity**

1.  First of all create a database to hold the passwords. Call it **ACCESS**.
    It consists of 2 fields only:
    ID – contains the user name or ID.
    PWORD – contains the password.
    Each field is 10 alphabetic characters long.

2.  Enter 2 records for two authorised users, **Andrew Main** and **Sally Chapman**:

    > ID = MAIN;  PWORD = GOLD
    >
    > ID = CHAPMAN;  PWORD = RUBY.

    Make sure that when you exit and save your database that **you have not** inadvertently appended a third blank record.
    If you do a user will be able to bypass the password system **by entering blanks** which will match those in the blank record.

3.  We will create a program to allow it to check the passwords in the ACCESS database.
    Copy the CUSTADD2 program, renaming it CUSTADD3.
    Add the following code to the start of CUSTADD3.

    *Do not run the program yet.*

    It will check that the user has a valid ID and password before allowing them to proceed with the rest of the program to add a new customer record.

    ```
    * CLEAR SCREEN
    CLEAR
    * CALL PASSWORD SCREEN
    * LOOP UNTIL USER ENTERS CORRECT PASSWORD
    DO WHILE .T.
        * INITIALISE VARIABLES FOR ID AND PASSWORD
        STORE SPACE (10) TO M_ID
        STORE SPACE (10) TO M_PWORD
        @ 2,14 SAY 'QUALITY WINES DATE:' + DTOC(DATE())
        @ 4,20 SAY 'PASSWORD ENTRY SCREEN'
        @ 8,10 SAY 'ENTER USER ID'
        @ 10,12 GET M_ID PICTURE '!!!!!!!!!!'
        @ 8,40 SAY 'ENTER PASSWORD'
        @ 10,42 GET M_PWORD PICTURE '!!!!!!!!!!'
        READ
        * CALL PASSWORD PROGRAM WITH 2 PARAMETERS
        DO PASSWORD WITH M_ID,M_PWORD
    ```

```
                    CLEAR
                    * CHECK THE PARAMETER PASSED BACK FROM PASSWORD
                    * PROGRAM
                    IF M_ID = 'NO'
                        CLEAR
                        LOOP
                    ELSE
                        EXIT
                    ENDIF
                ENDDO
                CLEAR
                * CONTINUE WITH MAIN PROGRAM
```

4.   The user, on calling the CUSTADD3 program, now gets an initial password
     screen and is prompted to enter two variables, M_ID and M_PWORD.
     These are read into the variables and another program – PASSWORD – is called,
     using the DO command.
     The 2 variables are passed to this program as parameters, using the WITH
     qualifier.
     As we will see shortly, this second program compares these parameters with
     records in the ACCESS database.
     If no match is found, one of the parameters is reset to 'NO', and passed back to
     the calling program CUSTADD3.
     The LOOP command starts the DO loop again, and the user is compelled to rekey.
     Otherwise the EXIT command terminates the DO loop and the rest of the
     program can continue – appending a customer record.

5.   After you have created the ACCESS database and the program ADDMEMB3,
     create the following program PASSWORD.PRG:

```
            * PROGRAM PASSWORD.PRG
            * < PROGRAMMER NAME/CREATION OR MODIFICATION DATE >
            * VALIDATES PARAMETERS USER ID AND PASSWORD
            * PASSED FROM CALLING PROGRAM
            PARAMETERS M_ID,M_PWORD
            SET TALK OFF
            * OPEN PASSWORD DATABASE
            USE ACCESS
            GO TOP
            * SEARCH FOR MATCH FOR 2 PARAMETERS
            LOCATE FOR M_ID = ID .AND. M_PWORD = PWORD
            IF .NOT. FOUND()
                STORE 'NO' TO M_ID
                SET COLOR TO +G*
```

WAIT 'INCORRECT ID OR PASSWORD – PRESS ANY KEY' TO MSG
ENDIF
SET COLOR TO
SET TALK ON
RETURN

The PARAMETERS command at line 5 receives the 2 parameters, the LOCATE command attempts to match them to the 2 records in the ACCESS database. The .AND. connector is used as both parameters must match. If the record is not found, one of the parameters is reset to 'NO' – it doesn't matter which. A flashing error message is displayed and control is returned to the calling program – in this case CUSTADD3.

The calling program now uses an IF condition to take further action. If the parameter is reset to 'NO', then the LOOP command compels the user to re-key. If the parameter is not reset then the EXIT command terminates the DO loop and the user can continue with the rest of the CUSTADD3 program and add a customer record.

6. Now run and test the CUSTADD3 program, making sure that the password and ID work correctly.

### Independent activities

1. Modify the main menu program MENU2.PRG that you created in Activity 1 to incorporate a password check.
Make sure that it calls CUSTADD3 now (the latest version), not CUSTADD2.

2. At the moment there is no way for users to exit if they fail to input their password and user ID successfully.
Amend the DO loop in the calling program so that the user automatically exits the program after the third unsuccessful attempt.

   *Hints:* you will have to set up a variable COUNTER and increment it every time the DO loop is executed.
   The DO loop will only execute WHILE this variable is less than 4.

3. Display a user message telling the user that he/she has made too many access attempts.

---
**Summary of commands used**
*DO < PROGRAM NAME > WITH < PARAMETER LIST >*
   Calls a program and passes named parameters to it
*PARAMETERS < PARAMETER LIST >*
   Lists the parameters that have been passed from a calling program.

# Activity 6 *Conclusion – bringing it all together*

## Objectives

1. To review the applications developed so far.
2. To place the applications on a menu.
3. To extend data validation routines and user choice to all programs.

## Introduction

If you have completed all the activities in this book then you have mastered the fundamentals of dBASE.

These are the major applications that you have created:

Databases:

| | | |
|---|---|---|
| | TRADCUST.DBF | Quality Wine's trade customers. |
| | TRADTRAN.DBF | Details of trade customer orders. |

Reports:

| | |
|---|---|
| TRANREP | Prints transactions from TRADTRAN |
| CREDREP | Prints customer credit details from TRADCUST. |

Queries/Views:

| | |
|---|---|
| VIEW1 | Calculates amount that customers exceed credit limit. |

Screen Formats

| | |
|---|---|
| CUSTSCRN | Data entry screen for TRADCUST. |
| TRANSCRN | Data entry screen for TRADTRAN. |

Programs:

| | | |
|---|---|---|
| 1. | CUSTADD3 | Adds a record to TRADCUST using password control. |
| 2. | CUSTED3 | Edits a TRADCUST record. |
| 3. | CUSTDEL3 | Deletes a TRADCUST record. |
| 4. | CUSTDET1 | Displays a customer record. |
| 5. | ADDTRAN1 | Adds a transaction record to TRADTRAN. |
| 6. | CREDLIST | Runs the CREDREP report. |
| 7. | CUSBAL1 | Updates customer balances in TRADCUST with transactions held in TRADTRAN. |
| 8. | ACDISP1 | Checks customers current credit balance from TRADCUST and unpaid orders from TRADTRAN. |
| 9. | MENU2 | Places programs 1- 5 above on a main menu. |
| 10. | PASSWORD | Validates user password and ID. |

**Independent activity**

1.  *Data Validation*

    Ensure that, where appropriate, data validation is extended to all the above programs, i.e.

    a.  Upper Case Conversion – see Chapter 7, Activities 4 and 5.

    b.  Range Checks – see Chapter 8, Activity 1.

    c.  Checks on data types, numeric and character – see Chapter 8, Activity 4.

2.  *User Choice*

    Incorporate the following choices in all the above programs, where appropriate.

    a.  Chance for the user to abort the program before proceeding with it – see Chapter 7, Activity 4.

    b.  Chance to cancel changes to the database, e.g. before the record is finally added, deleted or edited – see Chapter 7, Activity 5.

    c.  Chance to repeat the program – see Chapter 8, Activities 1 and 2.

    d.  If a program fails to find a record, then a 'not found' message is displayed and the user is given the chance to repeat.

3.  *Password Protection*

    Where a program allows users to amend records, as opposed to merely viewing them or printing a report, then password protection can be incorporated – see Chapter 8, Activity 5.

4.  *Extending the Main Menu*

    Programs numbered 1–5 on the above list should already be called from the main menu program MENU2.
    Extend the menu so that programs 6 – 8 can also be called.

# Index

*Any page numbers between 1 and 46 indicate coverage of dBASE III only, pages 47–102 indicate dBASE IV coverage and pages 103 onwards refer to both versions.*

# Paradox 4.0 for Students

*An Active-Learning Approach*

P M Heathcote

This book is aimed at any student of business or computing who needs to learn the basics of Borland's Paradox database (version 4.0), and will enable the student to set up and use any Paradox database.

It is known to be used on the following courses: HND Business and Finance, HND Computing, short courses/workshops, management and computing applications.

A lecturers' supplement is available in the form of two disks which contain the completed sample application together with the test data used in the book. The disk also contains, in a series of different directories, the state of the application as it should be at various key points, so that students who have forgotten, mislaid or corrupted their disks can be brought up to date without having to repeat stages already covered.

**Review comments**

*'A superb value book for use in hands-on computer teaching.'*

*'Easy to follow and understand ... students like the layout.'*

*'Excellent – 'project' orientation format useful to give systems perspective.'*     Lecturers

**1st edition • 224 pp • 245 x 190 mm • 1993 • 1 85805 042 1**

---

# MS Works

*An Active-Learning Approach*

D Weale

The aim of the book is to provide a 'user friendly' guide for students being introduced to spreadsheets, databases and word processing via MS Works.

It is known to be used on the following courses: GNVQ Intermediate and Higher, A Level Computing, Access to Computing, and the many courses requiring a basic knowledge of spreadsheets, databases and word processing via MS Works.

**Review comments**

*'A good coverage of the basics at a realistic price.'*

*'A first-class training course that leads to a high degree of operational efficiency.'*

Lecturers

**1st edition • 144 pp • 245 x 190 mm • 1992 • ISBN 1 873981 30 9**

# MS Access for Business Students
*An Active-Learning Approach*

S J Coles & J E Rowley

This book is intended for students on a wide variety of business studies and other courses who need to know how to use a straightforward, yet powerful, database package such as Access. It assumes no prior knowledge of databases.

**1st edition • 160 pp (approx) 245 x 190 mm • July 1994 • ISBN 1 85805 096 0**

---

# Word for Windows 2.0
*An Active-Learning Approach*

S J Coles & J E Rowley

This book is intended for students on a wide range of business and other courses who need to know how to use MS Word for Windows, one of the industry standard word processing packages.

It is known to be used on the following courses: BTEC National Computer Studies, Computer Applications, A Level Computing, HND Computing, HND Business and Finance, BTEC First IT.

**Review comments**

*'Excellent value – precise, to the point and easy to follow.'*

*'Exactly what's required.'*

*'An excellent book at a student-affordable price.'*                 Lecturers

**1st edition • 160 pp • 245 x 190 mm • 1993 • ISBN 1 85805 047 2**

---

# MS Works for Windows
*An Active-Learning Approach*

D Weale

This book provides an easy-to-follow, self-teaching text for students who need a good working knowledge of Works for Windows.

**1st edition • 208 pp • 245 x 190 mm • April 1994 • ISBN 1 85805 073 1**

# WordPerfect 6.0 for Windows

*An Active-Learning Approach*

E Leonard

This book not only provides a self-teaching text for any student needing to know how to use WordPerfect 6.0 for Windows, it also meets the wordprocessing requirements of all four levels of C&G 7261. As a result it is ideal for anyone for whom the basics of word-processing are a requirement.

**1st edition • 250 pp (approx) • 245 x 190 mm • July 1994 • ISBN 1 85805 097 9**

---

# PageMaker 4

*An Active-Learning Approach*

T Waters

This book is aimed at students on a wide variety of courses who want to know how to use Macintosh or PC versions of PageMaker 4.

It is known to be used on the following courses: GNVQ Adanced Business, A Level Computing, C&G 726, BTEC National Computer Studies, HNC/D Computer Studies.

**Review comments**

*'Excellent for self-paced work.'*

*'An excellent book for under £6. Very nicely structured. Easy to follow.'*          Lecturers

**1st edition • 208 pp • 245 x 190 mm • 1993 • ISBN 1 85805 065 0**

# Excel for Business Students

*Using Excel for Windows versions 3 & 4*

J Muir

This book is aimed at students who need to learn Excel 3 or 4 to acquire spreadsheet skills. Both Excel and its business applications are explained in simple terms, and the author has deliberately avoided biasing the examples towards areas where specialised knowledge of accountancy is required.

It is known to be used on the following courses: BA Business, Accounting Foundation courses, DMS, HND Computing, BTEC National Travel and Tourism, MSc Business IT, BTEC HND Business Studies, GNVQ Intermediate and Advanced Business.

**Review comments**

*'Excellent – the only authoritative text on the market.'*

*'Well explained and illustrated, with good examples.'*

*'Excellent course book that will be used extensively.'*

Lecturers

**1st edition • 192 pp • 245 x 190 mm • 1993 • ISBN 1 85805 029 4**

---

# SuperCalc 5

*An Active-Learning Approach*

P H Bassett

This book aims to enable business and computing students to develop skills in using the various SuperCalc commands and formulae, and an awareness of the possible applications of SuperCalc.

It is known to be used on the following courses: BTEC National Business and Finance, BTEC National Computer Studies, BMAI, A Level Computing, City & Guilds, BA Management/Business Studies, HNC/D Computing, open learning courses, BIS.

**Review comments**

*'Very well presented and easy to understand.'*

*'A very easy-to-follow book. Instructions are comprehensive. Even the novice student can gain experience fairly quickly.'*

*'Another excellent book from this series.'*

Lecturers

**1st edition • 320 pp • 245 x 190 mm • 1993 • ISBN 1 85805 048 0**

# dBASE for
# Business Students

## An Active-Learning Approach

## J. Muir

*Jim Muir is a Senior Lecturer in Business Computing at Bournemouth University. He has had wide experience in teaching IT skills at a variety of levels.*

DP Publications Ltd
Aldine Place
LONDON W12 8AW
1992

**nents**

*A CIP catalogue record for this book can be obtained from the British
Library*

ISBN 1 873981 16 3
Copyright J. Muir © 1992


First edition 1992
Reprinted 1994

Typeset by
    Kai Typesetting, Nottingham
Printed in Great Britain by
    The Guernsey Press Co Ltd